Old Hickory
A Life Sketch of Andrew Jackson

NATIONAL PORTRAIT GALLERY
TENNESSEE STATE MUSEUM

Old Hickory
A Life Sketch of Andrew Jackson

JAMES G. BARBER

with an introduction by
Robert V. Remini

Published by the
NATIONAL PORTRAIT GALLERY
Smithsonian Institution
Washington, D.C.

and by the
TENNESSEE STATE MUSEUM
Nashville

in association with the
UNIVERSITY OF WASHINGTON PRESS
Seattle and London

1990

This exhibition has been made possible in part through the support of the Tennessee General Assembly.

The Exhibition
National Portrait Gallery, Washington, D.C.
November 9, 1990, to January 13, 1991

Tennessee State Museum, Nashville
February 18 to April 28, 1991

Library of Congress Cataloging-in-Publication Number: 90-63011

ISBN: 0-295-97081-2

Above
Jackson's white beaver hat
Tennessee State Museum; Tennessee
Historical Society Collection

Cover illustration
Andrew Jackson (detail)
By Aaron H. Corwine (1802–1830)
Oil on canvas, 1825
69.9 x 55.9 cm. (27½ x 22 in.)
Mr. and Mrs. Jackson P. Ravenscroft

Frontispiece
Andrew Jackson
By Thomas Sully (1783–1872)
Oil on canvas, 1819
118.1 x 93.9 cm. (46½ x 37 in.)
New York State Office of Parks, Recreation
and Historic Preservation, Clermont State
Historic Site

CONTENTS

Engraving on cloth of The Glorious Victory of New Orleans
Historic New Orleans Collection; Museum/Research Center, Acc. No. 1947.19

FOREWORD

THE NATIONAL PORTRAIT GALLERY HAS DEDICATED SEVERAL OF ITS
special exhibitions over the past two years to topics related to the bicentennial
of the Constitution of the United States. These have included the portrayal of
the American colonists by the artists working in the New World; the legislative
branch, represented by the First Federal Congress; and the judicial branch,
explored through portraits of significant lawyers and judges. We turn now to
the executive branch of our government in this final exhibition of our
bicentennial series.

As we considered how to represent the presidency, it occurred to staff
historian James Barber that Andrew Jackson would provide an admirable
subject. Jackson's predecessors in the presidency had been leaders in the
Revolutionary War, drafters of the fundamental documents of the new nation,
members of the new "establishment" in America. Jackson, by contrast, was the
first President to emerge from the ordinary citizenry and to win the post in a
hotly contested election. It might be said that Jackson's presidency marked the
beginning of American politics as it is practiced today, with all of its strengths
and weaknesses.

The earlier Presidents had demonstrated their powers of judgment through
their leadership in the Revolutionary War, their involvement in the drafting
and ratifying of the Constitution, or their efforts in the first years of American
diplomacy. Jackson's appeal was that of a man of common sense, strength, and
determination. His predecessors had come from comfortable backgrounds.
Jackson came from humble circumstances farther south, and emerged as a
military hero after a somewhat checkered career in local and national politics.
The blemishes in his personal life were a godsend to his opponents, and his
shortcomings were portrayed vividly throughout the presidential campaign. Yet
Jackson manifestly captured the imagination and affection of the American
people.

His popularity can be measured by the demand for his portraits. Time and
again Jackson was asked to sit for large paintings, for miniatures, for drawings,
and (late in life) for photographs, and he acceded to these requests with a
patience that would be astonishing in a President today. Jackson appears to
have understood how much these depictions might reinforce his personal
popularity; whether he could have predicted how they would contribute to his
subsequent reputation is not as clear, but the fact remains that we "know" the
mature Jackson better than practically any of his contemporaries through the
extraordinary pictorial record of his appearance, his family, and his milieu.

I can think of no subject more appropriate for an exhibition at the National Portrait Gallery than Andrew Jackson, given his own recognition of the importance of portraiture in his career, and given the remarkable composite picture that emerges from the portraits for which he sat. All of us are grateful to James Barber for the insight and industry he has brought to bear on this book and for assembling the exhibition on which it is based. I join him in thanking the State of Tennessee, the Tennessee State Museum, the many lenders to the exhibition, and our colleagues who assisted so generously in this undertaking.

ALAN FERN
Director
National Portrait Gallery

PREFACE

ANDREW JACKSON! EVEN TODAY THAT NAME ENGENDERS AN immediate response from most Americans: the man on the twenty-dollar bill; the seventh President; the hero of New Orleans; the friend of the common man; a defender of his wife's reputation; duelist; soldier; the man most blamed for the Trail of Tears and the Panic of 1837, and most credited for the acquisition of Florida. Jackson was, and remains, a difficult person to define: part hero, part hellion, but wholly a man of the people and an icon in his own time.

That man and the various images of him are to be examined by the Tennessee State Museum and the National Portrait Gallery in this joint exhibition. In 1987, James C. Kelly, former chief curator at the Tennessee State Museum—and now at the Virginia Historical Society—and James G. Barber, historian at the National Portrait Gallery, began discussing the possibilities of bringing the exhibition to Nashville, Jackson's hometown. "Old Hickory: A Life Sketch of Andrew Jackson" not only commemorates the bicentennial of the United States presidency; it explores important aspects of Andrew Jackson's life, both public and private. We see him as husband, soldier, lawyer, politician, and statesman.

It is with great pleasure that the Tennessee State Museum once again works with the National Portrait Gallery. We jointly celebrated another noted Tennessean in 1986, in the exhibition "Davy Crockett: Gentleman from the Cane."

It is highly appropriate that "Old Hickory" is being shown in Washington and Nashville, the two cities where Jackson spent most of his life. We are greatly honored and pleased to take part in the exhibition.

LOIS RIGGINS EZZELL
Executive Director
Tennessee State Museum

ACKNOWLEDGMENTS

HOSPITALITY HAS BEEN THE ONE CHARACTER TRAIT OF ANDREW Jackson's that has consistently been demonstrated by the lenders to this exhibition and by those who have in other ways been entrusted with preserving his memory. In Nashville, James Kelly, former curator at the Tennessee State Museum (but now with the Virginia Historical Society), took an immediate interest in this exhibition in its formative stages, as did that institution's director, Lois Riggins Ezzell. For the Tennessee State Museum's generous support in cosponsoring and cofunding this project I am most appreciative. In this last regard, Donna Frost, the museum's development officer, put in many long hours.

At the Hermitage, Andrew Jackson's home outside of Nashville, I am especially grateful to Marsha Mullin, curator of the collection; to her assistant, Brenda Abernathy; and to historian Sharon Macpherson for their assistance in fielding research and loan requests.

I also owe William Cook my thanks and gratitude for sharing his expertise on Jacksonian iconography. Likewise, Merl Moore and Cheryl Kramer generously gave their assistance on other Jackson topics.

Elsewhere I received much-needed help from curators and historians alike, most especially Georgia Barnhill of the American Antiquarian Society; Lynda Heffley of City Hall, Charleston, South Carolina; David Cassidy and Linda Stanley of the Historical Society of Pennsylvania; Kathleen Johnson of Historic Hudson Valley; John Mahe of the Historic New Orleans Collection; Harold Moser, editor of the Jackson Papers Project; Kenneth Finkel of the Library Company of Philadelphia; John B. Harter of the Louisiana State Museum; Martha A. Sandweiss of the Mead Art Museum, Amherst College; James Rush and William Lind of the National Archives; Wendy Shadwell of the New-York Historical Society; and Betty Monkman at the White House. At the Smithsonian's National Museum of American History, Larry Bird, James Bruns, Donald Kloster, Anne Serio, and Butch Vosloh all gave timely assistance.

Within the Gallery itself, many staff members contributed their special talents. In the Office of Exhibitions, Beverly Cox and assistants Claire Kelly, Vandy Cook, and Cheryl Anderson deserve hearty recognition for supervising all of the many and necessary details that made this project possible. In other offices expeditious assistance was rendered by K. B. Basseches, Mary Blair Dunton, Daphne Greene, Martin Kalfatovic, Ann Shumard, Deborah Sisum, Patricia Svoboda, Penny Dwyer, Linda Thrift, and Rolland White. Director Alan Fern and Assistant Directors Marc Pachter and Carolyn Carr were all instrumental in guiding this exhibition to a successful completion. Special thanks are due the Gallery's editors, Frances Stevenson and Dru Dowdy, for their expenditure of time and attention in the preparation of this manuscript. I am also grateful to Michael Kammen, Smithsonian Regent's Fellow in 1990 at the Gallery, for his thoughtful comments.

Finally, the Gallery owes a special debt of gratitude to Professor Robert V. Remini, Jackson's distinguished biographer, for writing, upon short notice, the introduction.

JAMES G. BARBER

LENDERS TO THE EXHIBITION

American Antiquarian Society, Worcester, Massachusetts

The American Numismatic Society, New York, New York

Baltimore City Life Museums, Maryland

Blair House, Department of State, Washington, D.C.

Norman Brand

Cincinnati Art Museum, Ohio

City Hall Collection, Charleston, South Carolina

William L. Clements Library, University of Michigan, Ann Arbor

Columbia Museum of Art, South Carolina

The Corcoran Gallery, Washington, D.C.

Cummer Gallery of Art, Jacksonville, Florida

The Thomas Gilcrease Institute of American History and Art, Tulsa, Oklahoma

Gulf States Paper Corporation, Warner Collection, Tuscaloosa, Alabama

The Hermitage: Home of President Andrew Jackson, Hermitage, Tennessee

The Historical Society of Pennsylvania, Philadelphia

Historic Hudson Valley, Tarrytown, New York

Historic New Orleans Collection, Louisiana

The Library Company of Philadelphia, Pennsylvania

Library of Congress, Washington, D.C.

Louisiana State Museum, New Orleans

The Masonic Library and Museum of Pennsylvania, Philadelphia

Mead Art Museum, Amherst College, Amherst, Massachusetts

The Metropolitan Museum of Art, New York, New York

Merl M. Moore, Jr.

Museum of the City of New York, New York

National Archives, Washington, D.C.

National Gallery of Art, Washington, D.C.

National Museum of American Art, Smithsonian Institution, Washington, D.C.

National Museum of American History, Smithsonian Institution, Washington, D.C.

National Museum of the American Indian, Smithsonian Institution, Washington, D.C.

National Portrait Gallery, Smithsonian Institution, Washington, D.C.

Mr. and Mrs. John R. Neal

The New-York Historical Society, New York

New York State Office of Parks, Recreation and Historic Preservation, Clermont State Historic Site, Germantown

Pennsylvania Academy of the Fine Arts, Philadelphia

Private collections

Mr. and Mrs. Jackson P. Ravenscroft

Redwood Library and Athenaeum, Newport, Rhode Island

Sedalia Public Library, Missouri

Tennessee State Library and Archives, Nashville

Tennessee State Museum, Nashville

Travellers Rest Historic House Museum, Inc., Nashville, Tennessee

United States Naval Academy Museum, Annapolis, Maryland

The White House, Washington, D.C.

CHRONOLOGY

Porcelain vase with portrait of Andrew Jackson
The White House Collection

1767
March 15: Born, Waxhaw settlement, South Carolina

1780–1781
Participates in American Revolution; is captured and later released

1787–1788
Studies law and practices in North Carolina

1788
October: Arrives in Nashville

Circa 1791
Marries Rachel Donelson Robards

1791
February 15: Is appointed attorney general for the Mero District in Tennessee under the territorial government

1794
January 18: Remarries Rachel in a legal ceremony

1795
December 19: Is elected delegate to Tennessee Constitutional Convention

1796
October 22: Is elected to United States House of Representatives

1797
September: Is elected to United States Senate; resigns seat in 1798

1798
December 20: Is elected judge of Superior Court of Tennessee

1802
April 1: Is commissioned major general of Tennessee militia

1804
August 4: Purchases Hermitage property

1806
May 30: Kills Charles Dickinson in duel

1808
December: Adopts infant nephew; names him Andrew Jackson, Jr.

1814
March 27: Defeats Creek Indians at Horseshoe Bend, Mississippi Territory

May 28: Is commissioned major general in United States Army

August 9: Imposes Treaty of Fort Jackson on Creek Nation, thus ending Creek War

1815
January 8: Defeats British at New Orleans, ending War of 1812

March 31: Is fined one thousand dollars by Judge Dominick A. Hall for contempt of court

1817–1818
Befriends portrait painter Ralph E. W. Earl; assumes command of Seminole War in Spanish West Florida

1819
January–February: Visits Washington, D.C., to defend his conduct in Seminole War; visits major northeastern cities, where leading artists execute life portraits of him

Builds Hermitage mansion

1821
June 1: Appointed governor of Florida Territory; resigns from that office after eleven weeks

1823
October 1: Is elected to United States Senate

1824
Is nominated for President of the United States

March 16: Is presented gold medal voted by Congress, February 27, 1815, in recognition of his victory at New Orleans

1825
February 9: Is defeated for President in House of Representatives election

October 12: Resigns Senate seat

1828
November: Is elected President

December 22: Rachel dies suddenly

1829
March 4: Is inaugurated seventh President of the United States

1829–1830
Is troubled by Peggy Eaton scandal

1830
May 28: Signs Indian Removal Bill

1831
April: Accepts cabinet resignations and appoints new cabinet

December: Remodels Hermitage and builds tomb in garden

1832
July 10: Vetoes bill to recharter second Bank of the United States

November: Is reelected President

December 10: Issues Proclamation to the people of South Carolina warning against nullification

1834
March 28: Is censured by Senate for alleged abuse of executive powers

1835
January 30: Survives assassination attempt

1836
February: Concludes French spoliations claims controversy

1837
March 4: Issues farewell address and leaves office

1838
July 15: Joins Presbyterian Church, thus fulfilling promise made to Rachel in 1826

September 16: Ralph E. W. Earl dies at Hermitage

1840
January: Visits New Orleans to attend Silver Jubilee of his military victory on January 8, 1815

1842
Is troubled by debt and worsening health

1845
April: Is photographed at Hermitage

May 29: George P. A. Healy paints last life portrait of Jackson

June 8: Dies at Hermitage

June 10: Is buried in Hermitage garden beside Rachel

INTRODUCTION

*Ivory cameo brooch
of Andrew Jackson,
not dated.
National Museum
of American History,
Smithsonian
Institution*

IN THE OPINION OF SOME AMERICANS, ANDREW JACKSON WAS THE most popular man this nation had ever produced prior to the Civil War. George Washington, Thomas Jefferson, Patrick Henry, Benjamin Franklin, James Madison—all remarkable and beloved figures—could not compare to Old Hickory in their affections.

More popular than the "Father of His Country?" Could that be possible? Indeed so, Philip Hone, a New York merchant, confided to his diary in June 1833. President Jackson, he wrote, "is certainly the most popular man we have ever known. Washington was not so much so. His acts were popular . . . but he was superior to the homage of the populace, too dignified, too grave for their liking, and men could not approach him with familiarity." Although Hone opposed Jackson politically and preferred Henry Clay, he was forced to admit that the seventh President of the United States was "a *gourmand* of adulation . . . [and] no man ever lived in the country to whom the country was so much indebted. Talk of him as the second Washington! It won't do now; Washington was only the first Jackson."

Even after Old Hickory died, some men tried to vote for him for President during the crisis of 1860, as though by their collective vote they could raise him from the grave to help the nation escape the horrors of approaching disunion and civil war.

He was also a genuine celebrity. People came from miles around to see him when they heard that he might pass through their district. As his steamboat plied the Ohio River, taking him back and forth from his home in Tennessee to the capital, masses of shouting, waving, applauding people gathered along the river bank to call to him, salute him, and wish him success.

For his devoted followers, Andrew Jackson was the nation's finest image of itself during the first half of the nineteenth century. The original self-made man, he personified everything good and heroic and successful in American life. Although orphaned at an early age and burdened by poverty and a limited education, he rose to become a distinguished planter, lawyer, judge, military commander, and statesman.

Most important of all, Jackson won the Battle of New Orleans against tremendous odds. That victory alone enshrined him forever in the hearts of his countrymen. Throughout the War of 1812, the United States had suffered one military defeat after another. Its coastline was blockaded, its capital burned, its reputation besmirched throughout Europe. Some Americans actually feared for the survival of their experiment in liberty and republicanism.

Then came New Orleans. A rag-tagged conglomeration of militiamen, regular army enlistees, sailors, pirates, Indians, and a "colored battalion" met a superior force of invading British soldiers in a swampy area along the Mississippi River, just a short distance south of New Orleans. The Americans lined up behind a ditch that ran from the river to a cypress swamp, while the British army, in full regalia, with flags flying and martial music blaring, attacked. Wave after wave of redcoats assaulted the ditch. And wave after wave of British officers and men pitched to the ground, as the American sharpshooters picked them off one by one. As the "flashing and roaring hell" in front of them grew more intense, the invaders recoiled and then began a general retreat.

When the firing ceased and the Americans scaled the parapet protecting their ditch, the scene gave Jackson the "grand and awful" sense of what the resurrection might be like. "After the smoke of the battle had cleared off somewhat," he later wrote, "I saw in the distance more than five hundred Britons emerging from the heaps of their dead comrades, all over the plain, rising up, and still more distinctly visible as the field became clearer, coming forward and surrendering as prisoners of war to soldiers." The casualties among the British soldiers totaled 2,037; among Americans only 13 were killed, 39 wounded, and 19 missing in action.

It was a fantastic victory, the greatest feat of American arms in history up to that time. The British soldiers who had defeated Napoleon and forced his abdication had been decisively whipped by American regulars and frontiersmen who were fighting for their freedom and the security of their homeland.

Was it any wonder that General Andrew Jackson became the most beloved, admired, and respected man in the United States? He had restored to the American people their pride and self-confidence. Through his incredible victory, they had proved to the world the legitimacy of their independence, and that they could defend it against the mightiest power on earth. Never again did they need to prove to themselves or anyone else that they had a right to be free and independent. Americans alerted a hostile European world of kings and emperors that if they trifled with the sovereignty of the United States, they did so at their peril. Andrew Jackson had proven for all time the strength, vigor, and power of American life and institutions.

To a large extent, the extraordinary dimension of Jackson's military victory, as well as his success in overcoming personal handicaps and deficiencies, and in rising from the lowest to the highest social strata in the nation, resulted from unique character flaws and strengths. He was a complex of driving ambition, rigid personal discipline, strong loyalties, and ferocious hatreds. As commander of American forces at New Orleans, he demonstrated steely determination, supreme self-confidence, and extraordinary military skill, despite a near-total lack of experience or training. Later, as President of the United States, he displayed exceptional powers of understanding in grappling with national issues; an unshakable belief in the right of the American people to self-government; and an abiding love of the Union. As President he guided the country as it evolved inexorably from republicanism to democracy.

Jackson's parents had migrated to America from Carrickfergus, northern Ireland, in 1765, along with many other Scotch-Irish. Andrew and Elizabeth Hutchinson Jackson probably landed in Philadelphia and then moved southward to join relatives living in the Waxhaw settlement, located along the northwestern boundary separating North and South Carolina. They had two sons, Hugh and Robert, and they settled on land adjacent to the Twelve Mile Creek, a branch of the Catawba River. Then, in 1767, the father suddenly died, and not many weeks later Elizabeth gave birth to her third son on March 15, 1767, and named him after her late husband.

Elizabeth moved into the home of her sister, Jane Crawford, and her husband, where young Andrew and his brothers were raised. Since her sister was a semi-invalid, Elizabeth became housekeeper and nurse. Andrew received a meager education at an academy conducted by Dr. William Humphries and, a little later, at a school run by James Stephenson. He quit school with the outbreak of the American Revolution and accompanied Colonel William Richardson Davie, probably as a courier, during the attack on the British post of Hanging Rock. He was thirteen years of age at the time.

His older brother, Hugh, died after the Battle of Stono Ferry in 1780, probably from heat stroke, and shortly thereafter Andrew and his brother Robert were captured by the British and imprisoned at Camden. At the time of his capture, Andrew was ordered to clean a British officer's boots, which he refused to do. Infuriated, the officer raised his sword and struck Andrew with it, leaving a deep gash on the boy's head and across several fingers.

At Camden, the brothers contracted smallpox. Their mother arranged their release in exchange for British prisoners, but Robert died before they arrived home. Andrew recovered, his face slightly marked with the scars of the disease. During his recovery, Elizabeth journeyed to Charleston to nurse American prisoners of war held in prison ships, and died from cholera a few months later.

An orphan at fourteen years of age, Andrew resided with relatives for a short time, drifted from one job to another, and finally moved to Salisbury, North Carolina, in 1784, to study law at the office of Spruce MacCay, a distinguished trial lawyer of the day. After obtaining a license to practice law in North Carolina, Jackson and several companions decided to migrate to the western end of the state, to what is now Tennessee. He built a successful practice in Nashville, married Rachel Donelson Robards, and participated in the convention that wrote the constitution by which Tennessee won admission as a state in the Union.

Over six feet tall and extremely slender, his face long and accentuated by a sharp and jutting jaw, Jackson always carried himself with military stiffness. His bristly dark hair stood nearly as erect as the man himself, and his bright, intensely blue eyes instantly signaled whatever passion surged within his cadaverous body.

As an extremely capable and hard-working lawyer with ties on his wife's side to one of the most important families in Tennessee, Jackson entered politics and rose quickly within the political hierarchy, thanks in large measure to the strong support of William Blount, the former territorial governor. Jackson served as the state's first representative to the United States House of Representatives, and later as United States senator. Resigning from the Senate after a single session, Jackson accepted appointment to the Tennessee Superior Court, where he served for six years. One biographer later described his decisions as a judge as "short, untechnical, unlearned, sometimes ungrammatical, and generally right."

Copper lusterware pitcher with image of Andrew Jackson. National Museum of American History, Smithsonian Institution

Jackson supplemented his income from time to time by running a general store. He even sold boats to Aaron Burr without fully comprehending Burr's scheme to undertake a military operation down the Mississippi River, for which Burr was later tried and acquitted of treason.

When war broke out with Great Britain in 1812, Jackson had won election as major general of the Tennessee militia because of his popularity among the field officers of the militia and a considerable amount of politicking he accomplished beforehand. Despite a lack of military experience, he quickly developed into an excellent commanding general, and his men affectionately dubbed him "Old Hickory," because he was a tough, but caring, officer. He sometimes made impossible demands on his men, but he constantly showed them that he would work unceasingly for their safety and well-being.

The governor of Tennessee sent Jackson and his militia against the Creek Indians in 1813, after they had attacked American settlers along the southern frontier. Old Hickory decisively defeated the Indians at the Battle of Horseshoe Bend on March 27, 1814, wrested twenty-three million acres of land from the Creek Nation under the terms of the Treaty of Fort Jackson, and then hurried to New Orleans in time to repel a British invasion and inflict a devastating defeat upon the enemy. A few years later, he pursued the Seminole Indians into Florida and seized control of the area from Spanish authority. His actions triggered an international crisis, involving England as well as Spain, because of his execution of two British subjects, Alexander Arbuthnot and Robert Ambrister, for aiding and abetting Indian attacks against American settlers. The United States, nevertheless, succeeded in purchasing Florida from the Spanish and obtaining a western boundary for the Louisiana Territory that extended to the Pacific Ocean. By this single action, the United States was transformed into a potential transcontinental power.

In 1821 Jackson served as territorial governor of Florida for a short period in order to officiate at the transfer of ownership from Spain to the United States and establish civil government. Despite arbitrary actions and an impatience with Spanish temperament, Jackson provided an energetic and efficient government that facilitated the transition of a foreign land into the American political system.

As the most popular and beloved man in the nation, Jackson received a nomination from the Tennessee legislature to run for the presidency. The legislature also seated him in the United States Senate, where he again served a short term. Despite a popular and electoral plurality in the presidential election of 1824, he did not receive the constitutionally mandated majority of electoral votes. The choice of President was therefore decided in the House of Representatives in a contest between Jackson, Secretary of State John Quincy Adams, and Secretary of the Treasury William H. Crawford. The Speaker of the House, Henry Clay, regarded Jackson as a military chieftain who had very limited qualifications to serve as President, and he therefore threw his considerable support to Adams. The House election ended on the first ballot, with Adams chosen as President.

Plate with image of Jackson. National Museum of American History, Smithsonian Institution

When Adams selected Clay as his secretary of state, Jackson exploded in indignation. He charged the two men with arranging a "corrupt bargain" in which Clay gave Adams sufficient votes in the House election to become President in return for appointment to the office of Secretary of State. Jackson resigned his Senate seat, returned to Tennessee, and began a campaign to win election to the presidency in 1828. With the help of Martin Van Buren and John C. Calhoun, he orchestrated the formation of an organization to support his election, which eventually became the Democratic party. With his popularity and the strength of his organization, and after a particularly vicious and sordid campaign—possibly the worst in American history for slander and misrepresentation—Jackson won a spectacular victory in 1828.

Jackson's tenure as President—1829 to 1837—extended over a period in which the United States underwent enormous political, economic, and cultural changes, changes by which the nation slowly began to emerge as an industrial democracy. In instituting what he called a program of "reform retrenchment and economy," President Jackson attempted to establish democratic government. He saturated the language of his messages to Congress and other state papers with democratic intent. "The people are sovereign," he repeated many times, "their will is absolute." His philosophy of government preached the simple message that the people govern, and that majority rule constitutes the only true means of preserving a free society.

A just government, declared Jackson in his celebrated veto of the bill to recharter the second National Bank of the United States, showers "its favors alike on the high and the low, the rich and the poor." He opposed government for and by an elite. "Every man is equally entitled to protection by law, but when the laws undertake . . . to make the rich richer and the potent more powerful, the humble members of society—the farmers, mechanics, and laborers— . . . have a right to complain of the injustice of their Government."

To advance his democratic ideals, he instituted what he called a program of rotation of office to bring in new blood and fresh ideas for the operation of government. No one has a vested right to government employment, he contended. His enemies, however, accused him of introducing a "spoils system" to Washington. As the Democratic senator from New York, William L. Marcy, boldly announced: "To the victor belong the spoils of the enemy."

Despite his democratic contentions, Jackson also expanded presidential powers during his tenure through his creative use of the veto (he vetoed more times than all of his predecessors put together) and his leadership of Congress and the Democratic party. He effectively intruded into the legislative process and materially increased the power of the chief executive to control and direct the operation of Congress.

One of Jackson's most unique contributions to constitutional ideas about the government and its operation was his belief that the Union was indivisible. In his Proclamation of December 10, 1832, written to the people of South Carolina after the state's convention had nullified the tariff laws of the country and threatened secession, he responded with the doctrine of the Union as a *perpetual* entity. He was the first American statesman to publicly declare that secession could not be invoked by any state to redress a supposed grievance. "Those who told you that you might peaceably prevent" the execution of federal law, he wrote, "deceived you. . . . Their object is disunion. But be not deceived by names. Disunion by armed force is *treason*. Are you ready to incur its guilt?" South Carolina ultimately backed down, and bloody civil war was postponed for nearly thirty years.

Jackson's extraordinary understanding of what is meant by "the United States" convinced Abraham Lincoln of the soundness of its constitutional argument. President Lincoln extracted from this Proclamation the basic justification he needed for his course of action to meet the secession crisis of 1861.

To Jackson's credit goes the distinction of having paid off the national debt. He had made the liquidation of the debt one of the goals of his administration, and he lived to see it happen in January 1835. It remains the only instance in American history when the nation owed nothing to anyone.

On a less happy note, the Jackson administration inaugurated the tragic history of Indian removal. The continued presence of the tribes within the several states caused mounting difficulties, including the shedding of blood, and had long defied solution by the national government. Thomas Jefferson hoped that through education the Indian might be integrated into white society. Failing that, he said, the tribes must be removed to the Rocky Mountains.

But many Indians resisted the idea of becoming cultural white men. They wished to remain as Indians, subject to Indian law, and preserving their heritage, language, and religion. The Cherokee Nation, for example, refused to obey Georgia law even though a large number of its people lived within the boundaries of that state.

Jackson contended that removal, such as Jefferson had suggested, would benefit both whites and Indians. It would prevent the annihilation of the Indian race, for one thing. More importantly, as far as Jackson was concerned, it would provide a greater degree of national security. Past Indian attacks, such as the Creek War just prior to the British invasion at New Orleans, jeopardized the safety of the American people. So Jackson prevailed upon Congress to pass the Indian Removal Act of 1830, by which lands held by the tribes within the states were exchanged for lands west of the Mississippi in an Indian territory that later became the state of Oklahoma. The government provided the transportation, but the removal turned into a death march because of the indifference and greed of those charged with executing it. The tribes were hastened along what the Cherokee called "The Trail of Tears." Thousands died along the way, and the entire operation disgraced the nation and blackened its history.

In foreign affairs, Jackson pursued an aggressive policy to force European governments to respect the integrity, sovereignty, and independence of the United States. Debts owed to the United States and incurred during the Napoleonic Wars had long been a source of irritation, because the European nations refused to pay what they legitimately owed. Jackson demanded payment and succeeded in bringing about settlement of the claims. He nearly provoked war with France over the settlement, but the dispute was ultimately resolved with the payment by the French government of twenty-five million francs. Jackson also settled claims against Denmark, Spain, and the Kingdom of Naples.

25th Anniversary of the Battle of New-Orleans ribbon. Historic New Orleans Collection; Museum/Research Center, Acc. No. 1974.67

Of particular value and importance to the United States was the conclusion of a treaty with Great Britain that resolved a long-standing dispute over trade with the West Indies. The treaty opened West Indian ports to the United States on terms of full reciprocity. The Jackson administration also signed the first treaty with an Asian nation in 1833, when Siam agreed to American trade on the basis of a most favored nation, a principle that became the basis of other treaties with South American countries and other Near Eastern countries.

After serving two terms as President, and designating Martin Van Buren as his successor, Jackson retired to his home at the Hermitage, just outside Nashville. For the remainder of his life, he took an active interest in national affairs. He favored the annexation of Texas and Oregon, even at the risk of war. And he helped his protégé, James K. Polk, win the Democratic nomination in 1844. The narrow victory of Polk in the election over Jackson's longtime enemy, Henry Clay, on a platform that called for the reannexation of Texas and reoccupation of Oregon, delighted the gravely ill old hero of New Orleans. "I thank my god," he wrote, "that the Republic is safe & that he had permitted me to live to see it, & rejoice."

Jackson died at the Hermitage at the age of seventy-eight on June 8, 1845, most likely from a heart attack. But he suffered so many different ills, acquired in the service of his country (as he liked to say), that modern physicians who delve into such matters are reluctant to pinpoint the exact cause of death. He was buried next to his beloved wife in the garden adjacent to his home.

ROBERT V. REMINI
Wilmette, Illinois

Old Hickory
A Life Sketch of Andrew Jackson

CHAPTER 1

Before Glory

ANDREW JACKSON'S HUMBLE BEGINNINGS IN THE CAROLINA BACK-country belied a distinguished future. His youthful predilection for gambling, cockfighting, horse racing, and tavern whiskey were in themselves obstacles to success. Then, too, Jackson had a sensitive nature and a volatile temper, the combinations of which disposed him on several occasions to risk longevity on the field of honor. Controversy was an integral facet of Jackson's character that he never outgrew. "Every step he took was a contest," declared one former adversary, and "every contest a victory."

In the fall of 1788, when Jackson reached Nashville, then a stockaded village of log cabins, he was intent upon practicing law. His sense of justice served him well in this profession: in 1791 he was appointed attorney general for the Mero District, and in 1798 he was elected judge of the Superior Court of Tennessee. Jackson earned a reputation for dispensing justice quickly, at times dispatching several dozen cases in a few days.

The fierce passions of Jackson's personal life, however, tarnished his image in the public eye. For instance, his impulsive marriage to Rachel Donelson Robards in 1791, before it was discovered that she had not yet been legally divorced, haunted the couple for the rest of their lives. More troublesome was the bullet that Charles Dickinson embedded next to Jackson's heart in a duel in 1806. Unlike Dickinson, Jackson escaped with his life, but his health was forever impaired. If a measure of foolhardy pluck flowed in Jackson's Scotch-Irish veins, so did a stubborn pride. His will to make something of himself early in life would in later years mature into a profound sense of duty to his country.

Rachel Jackson

Unknown to the happy young couple—Rachel (1767–1828) and Andrew Jackson—their wedding ceremony, in about 1791, was an irregular affair, one that Jackson's political adversaries touted as a national scandal in the 1828 presidential election. The trouble stemmed from Rachel's unfortunate first marriage in 1785 to Lewis Robards, a jealous spouse who suspected her affections. While he was resolving his suspicions, he banished Rachel back to her family's home on the Cumberland River, ten miles from Nashville. There Andrew Jackson found lodging upon his arrival in the city in 1788, and there he first gazed into the "lustrous dark eyes" of Rachel. Apparently she was guilty of nothing more flirtatious than polite sociability with Jackson or anyone else. But no one could convince Robards of this, and in 1790 he sued for divorce, the final proceedings of which he inexplicably delayed for two years. Later, when Andrew and Rachel discovered that their own marriage had been premature, they shamefully endured a second legal ceremony in 1794.

The circumstances of their union never poisoned their hearty affection for each other. Still, Rachel, a pious woman, suffered profound mortification until her death in 1828, which Jackson, having just been elected President, blamed on the innuendoes of scurrilous politicians. As a measure of his love, he allegedly wore this large miniature of Rachel around his neck, suspended by a strong black cord. During Jackson's presidency, Louisa Catherine Strobel painted this likeness after a portrait by Ralph E. W. Earl.

Louisa Catherine Strobel (1803–1883), after Ralph E. W. Earl
Watercolor on ivory, circa 1831
6.4 x 5.1 cm. (2½ x 2 in.)
The Hermitage: Home of President Andrew Jackson

John Overton

Given Jackson's headstrong temperament, which all too often left people shaking their fists, he was fortunate to have counted John Overton (1766–1833) among his circle of friends. Slight of build and quiet by nature, Overton had been the perfect foil for Jackson ever since the two young lawyers had shared a bunk at the home of Mrs. John Donelson, the widowed mother of Rachel Robards. Although not quite a year older, Overton acted like a big brother in counseling his friend about law and politics and even about Jackson's growing interest in the vivacious daughter of the landlady.

In 1794 the two men formed a partnership for the purchase and sale of some fifty thousand acres of land in western Tennessee; on part of this tract was founded the city of Memphis. Then in 1804, when Jackson resigned from the bench of the Tennessee Superior Court, Overton succeeded him. By the end of his distinguished legal career, Overton was the recognized state authority on land legislation. Not surprisingly, his own successful speculations made him the richest citizen in the commonwealth. Overton spent much of his retirement in the 1820s promoting Jackson's presidential candidacy and defending his maligned character.

Attributed to Ralph E. W. Earl
(circa 1788–1838)
Oil on canvas, circa 1820
71.1 x 59.7 cm. (28 x 23½ in.)
Travellers Rest Historic House Museum, Inc.

John Sevier

In 1798, John Sevier (1745–1815), the
first governor of Tennessee, signed a
proclamation appointing Jackson a judge
of the state superior court. Then in 1802,
and indicative of his growing popularity
and leadership abilities, Jackson was
elected major general of the Tennessee
militia over Sevier, whose hold on the
governorship had temporarily ended.
This was not an inconsequential feat for a
young jurist with virtually no military
experience. On the other hand, Sevier, a
veteran of the Revolution, was a hero of
the Battle of King's Mountain in 1780.
Appointed a brigadier general in 1791 to
defend the Southwest Territory, Sevier
proved to be an intrepid Indian fighter.
His successful forays against the Cherokee
all but broke the will of that proud nation.
At its conclusion, Sevier's military record
spoke for itself—thirty-five battles, thirty-
three victories.

As is often the case with ambitious men,
Jackson and Sevier were too much alike to
get along. In an attempt to squelch Sevier's
chances of running again for governor in
1803, Jackson leaked information
implicating Sevier in a land fraud involving
millions of acres in Tennessee. Sevier
ducked the charge and then leveled a blow
of his own—a public slur about Jackson
having run off with another man's wife.
The incident later led to a clumsy and
harmless duel. Thereafter the two antagon-
ists ignored their differences, each resum-
ing his own political ambitions.

Charles Willson Peale (1741–1827)
Oil on canvas, 1790–1792
73.6 x 62.2 cm. (29 x 24½ in.)
Tennessee State Museum; Tennessee
Historical Society Collection

Russell Bean surrendering to Judge Jackson

The real facts of this incident have eluded documentation, but the story of Judge Jackson's subduing Russell Bean, an excitable gunsmith, became a favorite anecdote told and retold in a variety of mediums for nearly half a century. According to one version, Andrew Jackson was holding court one day in a small Tennessee village when "a great hulking fellow, armed with pistol and bowie knife, took it upon himself to parade before the shanty court house, and cursed the judge, jury, and all there assembled, in set terms." Jackson immediately ordered the sheriff to arrest this scoundrel, Russell Bean, but neither he nor a posse were successful. There-upon Jackson adjourned court for ten minutes, walked into the street where Bean was "blaspheming at a terrible rate," and confronted him with loaded pistols. "Now," demanded Jackson, looking Bean straight in the eye, "surrender, you infernal villain, this very instant, or I'll blow you through!" A few days afterward, Bean was asked why he chose to submit. He explained that upon looking Jackson in the eye he "saw shoot, and there wasn't shoot in nary other eye in the crowd."

Unidentified artist
Engraving, not dated
11.1 x 15.9 cm. (4⅜ x 6¼ in.)
From the original in The New-York Historical Society

Matched .66-caliber dueling pistols, in case with accessories, formerly owned by Andrew Jackson

This saw-handle grip design was popular in the early 1800s.

National Museum of American History, Smithsonian Institution

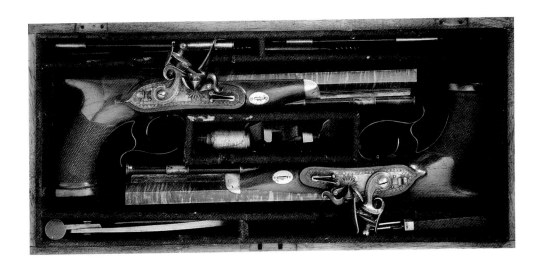

CHAPTER 2

The Iron General

JACKSON'S DISTINCTION IN AMERICAN MILITARY ANNALS RESTS NOT on his brilliance as a commander or as a tactician, but rather on his resolute determination to defeat an enemy at all costs. For his toughness in the field, his troops called him Old Hickory, a nickname that, in one way or another, he would live up to for the rest of his life. In the Creek War of 1813–1814, provoked by a massacre of white settlers at Fort Mims near Mobile, then a part of the Mississippi Territory, Jackson time and again demonstrated a will of iron. At the start of the campaign, he dragged himself out of a sickbed to rally Tennessee's volunteers and militia. Once on the field of battle, Jackson overcame a lack of food and supplies and troop desertions to strike the enemy a lethal blow at Horseshoe Bend. This crucial engagement exhausted the Indians' will to fight, just when the British were about to land troops in the South and supply the natives with vast stores of guns and ammunition.

The Treaty of Fort Jackson, imposed by Jackson himself in August 1814, severely punished the entire Creek nation, including those Indians who had remained friendly. Some twenty million acres of land, roughly three-fifths of the present state of Alabama and one-fifth of Georgia, were ceded to the United States. Westerners could now build roads and traverse virtually unimpeded from Tennessee to Mobile. Now the name of Andrew Jackson was no longer associated with just the rough-and-tumble of the frontier but with victory and honor. The federal government bestowed its laurels by commissioning Jackson a major general in the United States Army and assigning him the Seventh Military District. This was a southern command, and although it was not considered to be important at the time, subsequent British operations thrust at New Orleans late in 1814 placed the crux of America's defense in Jackson's hands.

Map of General Jackson's campaign against the Creek Indians, 1813 and 1814

John Coffee

Loyalty always meant a lot to Andrew Jackson, and there was no loyalty like that of a soldier. Jackson always considered John Coffee (1722–1833) to be his best friend; not surprisingly, Coffee had been Old Hickory's commander of cavalry in three wars. Actually, their relationship went back to 1804, when Jackson, along with his wife's nephew, John Hutchings, entered into a business partnership with Coffee to sell dry goods. The firm prospered for a time. Jackson eventually sold out to Coffee, who married one of his wife's many nieces. It was said that on Coffee's wedding day, Jackson magnanimously tore his notes of debt into pieces and presented them to the bride.

Coffee was a big man, stoutly built and well over six feet in height. On horseback he cut a formidable figure, but one not lacking in natural ease and grace. His cavalry command, however, was another story. During the Battle of New Orleans, in contrast to the primly uniformed British redcoats, his men, mostly shaggy and unshaven, presented a motley array of homespun and buckskin. In 1813 Coffee's defeat of the Creek Indians at Talluschatches proved to be one of the few American victories early in the war. Later, deserted by his volunteers, Coffee, although wounded in battle, stood by Jackson until the end of the victorious campaign. In 1815, upon Jackson's recommendation, Coffee was one of three American commissioners appointed by President James Monroe to survey the boundary established by the Treaty of Fort Jackson.

Jackson kept this portrait of Coffee on display at the Hermitage.

Attributed to Ralph E. W. Earl
(circa 1788–1838)
Oil on canvas, circa 1825
73.7 x 60.9 cm. (29 x 24 in.)
The Hermitage: Home of President Andrew Jackson

Jackson offering to share His Acorns with the soldier

One of the oft-told anecdotes of Jackson's military career was an incident that occurred during the Creek War. At a time when supplies were critically low and the army was existing on tripe, a gaunt soldier approached Jackson one morning while he was sitting under a tree eating, and begged for some food. "It has always been a rule with me," replied Jackson, "never to turn away a hungry man when it was in my power to relieve him, and I will most cheerfully divide with you what I have." Thereupon Jackson reached into his pocket, drew forth a few acorns, and shared them with the soldier. The astonished man circulated his story among his comrades, and it eventually appeared in newspapers throughout the country.

H. Hillyard and A. B. Cross (active in New York early 1840s)
Engraving, not dated
16.5 x 11.1 cm. (6½ x 4⅜ in.)
The New-York Historical Society

Interview Between Gen. Jackson & Weatherford

William Weatherford (circa 1780–1824), known as Chief Red Eagle, was the leader of the militant Creek Indians of the Mississippi Territory, who resisted all contact with white settlers as a means of preserving their own native culture. Inevitably, they grappled with encroachment upon their land, until hostile retaliation seemed to be the only solution. On August 30, 1813, Weatherford, himself of mixed blood, led his warriors in what became a massacre of nearly 250 whites at Fort Mims. Although he personally disapproved of the slaughter of women and children, Weatherford could not control his angry warriors.

Instigated by the Fort Mims massacre, the Creek War virtually ended with Jackson's victory at Horseshoe Bend on March 27, 1814. Weatherford was conspicuously absent from that engagement. Jackson wanted his capture most of all and directed the defeated chiefs to bring Weatherford to him. Jackson was astonished when Weatherford walked freely into his camp one day to make peace. "I am in your power," replied Weatherford. "Do with me as you please. . . . I can now do no more than weep over the misfortunes of my nation." Jackson was so taken with the Indian's courage and forthright plea for reconciliation that he released him, so that Weatherford might convince others to surrender.

John R. Chapin and W. Ridgway
(active 1854–1860)
Engraving, 1859
13.5 x 18.9 cm. (5⁵⁄₁₆ x 7⁷⁄₁₆ in.)
National Portrait Gallery, Smithsonian Institution

Thomas Pinckney

Jackson was fortunate to have had Major General Thomas Pinckney (1750–1828) as his superior officer in the Creek War. By nature, Pinckney was prudent, patient, and judicious. He was a veteran of the Revolution, a former governor of South Carolina, and an experienced foreign diplomat. In accepting command of the Sixth Military District, extending from North Carolina to the Mississippi River, Pinckney was ending a distinguished career of public service. For the militarily ambitious Jackson, his commander was not a rival but a friend.

In the Creek War, Pinckney did not see active duty, but instead carefully monitored his subordinates. Jackson proved to be the only one to distinguish himself. "Without the personal firmness, popularity, and exertions of that officer," Pinckney wrote, "the Indian war, on the part of Tennessee, would have been abandoned, at least for a time." Pinckney recommended Jackson's promotion to major general in the United States Army, which Jackson accepted on June 8, 1814. At the conclusion of the war, Jackson—voicing the sentiments of many westerners, who felt that the treaty terms, arranged in part by Pinckney, did not concede enough Indian territory to the United States—replaced his former superior as a peace commissioner.

Samuel F. B. Morse (1791–1872)
Oil on canvas, 1818
121.9 x 96.5 cm. (48 x 38 in.)
Anonymous loan to the Columbia Museum of Art

Treaty of Fort Jackson

On August 9, 1814, Old Hickory imposed the Treaty of Fort Jackson on the Creek Nation, officially ending approximately nine months of hostilities. Ironically, of the thirty-five chiefs who signed the treaty, only one was a member of the hostile Creek called Red Sticks. Although the government stipulated that the Indians should pay only indemnities for the cost of the war, which Jackson calculated to be more than twenty million acres of land, Jackson imposed such punitive demands as the right to build roads and military and trading posts throughout their domain. As a means of isolating them from British and Spanish influences in West Florida, Jackson ordered their removal from southern Georgia and from what is now central Alabama. In effect, the Treaty of Fort Jackson decimated the Creek and set a precedent for Indian removal to remote western lands for the rest of the nineteenth century.

National Archives

Pushmataha

Pushmataha (circa 1765–1824) was an influential Choctaw chief, well respected among his own people and a friend to the white man. Yet he represented, better than most Native Americans, the cruel plight of all Indian nations at the mercy of Andrew Jackson and the United States government. As allies, he and his warriors had joined ranks with Jackson in three wars—against the Creek, the British, and the Spanish. Then in 1820, Jackson, acting as a representative of his government, imposed the Treaty of Doak's Stand, which ceded to the United States more than five million acres of prime land belonging to the Choctaw, in what is now west central Mississippi.

On the treaty ground, Pushmataha accused his old friend of deception; the territory west of the Mississippi River that was being offered in exchange was essentially barren wasteland, he argued. At first, Jackson cajoled the Indians with disclaimers. Next, he bullied them with threats of military reprisals if they refused to remove, until finally Pushmataha and his fellow tribesmen had no recourse but to submit.

In 1824, Pushmataha visited Washington, where he met the Marquis de Lafayette, and was an attraction himself. This portrait by Charles Bird King was painted during his visit, shortly before he fell ill and died, and was ceremoniously buried in Congressional Cemetery in Washington, D.C.

Charles Bird King (1785–1862)
Oil on panel, 1824
44.5 x 34.9 cm. (17½ x 13¾ in.)
The Warner Collection of Gulf States Paper Corporation

CHAPTER 3

Hero of New Orleans

BY NOON OF JANUARY 8, 1815, WITH THE GUNS OF BATTLE MERCI-fully quiet on the plain of Chalmette some five miles from the city of New Orleans, Major General Andrew Jackson stood triumphant over a cane field, silver with frost that morning but now littered with the dead and wounded of George III's red-coated army. Among the dead, and symbolic of the British defeat, lay the commanding general, Sir Edward Michael Pakenham. The monthlong campaign had taken its toll on the forty-seven-year-old Jackson as well. Although the enemy refused to retreat immediately after that day's action, its eventual departure from Lake Borgne signaled victory for the Americans, and brought to a close the protracted War of 1812.

Jackson returned to the city a savior and a hero. In the days and weeks that followed, news of his stunning triumph rippled throughout the country, and the name of Andrew Jackson became known to all. The nation wanted a look at this American Napoleon, but scarcely a crude portrait or an engraving of him was known to exist at the time. This dearth of imagery would not persist. Artists, sculptors, friends, and admirers began asking Jackson for his likeness, which today is as common as a twenty-dollar bill.

A Correct View of the Battle Near the City of New Orleans

Public fascination with Jackson's New Orleans victory inspired numerous artistic renderings of the battle. *A Correct View of the Battle Near the City of New Orleans* was the work of Francisco Scacki; this crude production was said to have been his first and last attempt at engraving. Scacki experimented with a variety of techniques—etching, stipple and line engraving, roulette, and aquatint. But not even a barrage of methods could satisfy him with the first strike. Not wishing to waste precious paper, he printed a second state on the reverse. This time, however, he added five figures, which are plainly set off by the surrounding patches of white, the result of his first having had to burnish the plate smooth before reengraving it. In addition, Scacki enhanced the appearance of the battle smoke over the American rampart at the top. He also introduced an identification key on each side in the bottom margin.

Francisco Scacki (active 1815–1816)
Etching, engraving, aquatint, and soft ground on paper, circa 1816
40.6 x 60.5 cm. (16 x 23¹³⁄₁₆ in.)
National Portrait Gallery, Smithsonian Institution

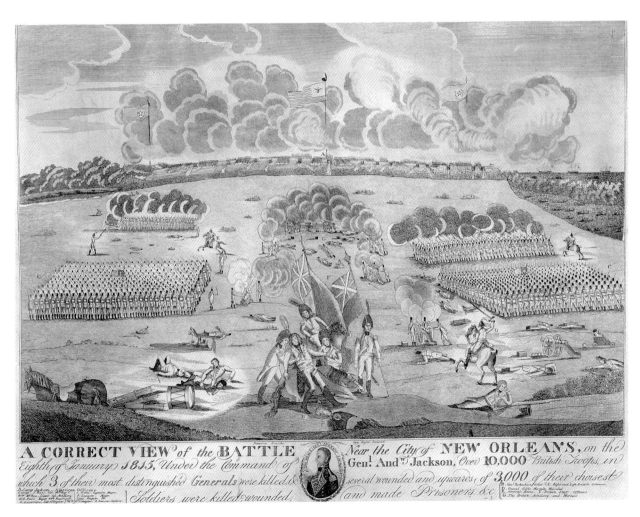

The Glorious Victory of New Orleans

R. Gray and Todd (active circa 1817)
Engraving on cloth, circa 1817
55.9 x 66.3 cm. (22 x 26⅛ in.)
Historic New Orleans Collection; Museum/
Research Center, Acc. No. 1947.19

**United States Army officer's coat
with epaulets, worn by General
Jackson**

National Museum of American History,
Smithsonian Institution

Gold medal presented to Jackson "as a testimony of the high sense entertained by Congress of his judicious and distinguished conduct"

On February 27, 1815, the United States Congress unanimously voted its thanks to Major General Jackson for his victory in New Orleans and resolved that the President have a gold medal struck with emblems of the splendid achievement. Moritz Fürst, a die-sinker trained in Vienna, engraved the medal, which bears a profile of Jackson on the obverse. The reverse, designed by Philadelphia portraitist Thomas Sully, allegorically depicts Victory and Peace, the former writing "Orleans" on a tablet while the other extends a restraining hand. However eager Congress was to extend its thanks, nine years passed before Jackson's medal was finished. Finally, on March 16, 1824, one day after his fifty-seventh birthday, Jackson received his medal from President James Monroe in a simple ceremony inside the presidential mansion.

Jackson's gold medal was allegedly discovered in a pawnshop. A number of bronze replicas were also stamped. As late as 1885, Charles E. Barber, chief engraver at the Philadelphia Mint, reported that Fürst's original dies were still in use.

Moritz Fürst (born 1782)
Gold, 1824
6.4 cm. (2½ in.) diameter
The American Numismatic Society

Andrew Jackson
by Jean François de Vallée

After Jackson's victory of January 8, 1815,
Jean François de Vallée, a French artist
living in New Orleans, painted an ivory
miniature of the hero. This likeness, and
an oil on canvas executed by Nathan
Wheeler at about this time, are the two
earliest extant portraits of Andrew
Jackson. According to Jackson biographer James Parton: *It is so unlike the
portraits familiar to the public, that not a man
in the United States would recognize in it the
features of General Jackson. Abundant,
reddish-sandy hair falls low over the high,
narrow forehead, and almost hides it from
view. . . . Eyes of a remarkably bright blue.
Complexion fair, fresh and ruddy. . . . The
miniature reminds you of a good country
deacon out for a day's soldiering.*

Before Jackson left New Orleans that
spring for his home in Tennessee, he
presented the miniature to Edward
Livingston. A man of talent and
diplomacy, Livingston had met Jackson
in 1796, when they had both served in
Congress. Originally from New York,
Livingston now made his home in New
Orleans, and became Jackson's military
secretary, aide-de-camp, interpreter,
confidant, and legal adviser.

Jean François de Vallée (active in New
Orleans 1808–1818)
Watercolor on ivory, 1815
7.6 x 6.4 cm. (3 x 2½ in.)
Historic Hudson Valley

Andrew Jackson
by Nathan W. Wheeler

The most prevalent and popular likenesses of the hero of New Orleans were crude engravings, many of which were inspired by this oil painting by Nathan W. Wheeler. A native of Massachusetts, Wheeler was a veteran of the battle of January 8, 1815, and afterward made his living as a distiller and artisan painter, principally in New Orleans. Early in May 1815, notice of Wheeler's portrait of Jackson appeared in the *Louisiana Gazette.* The artist advertised to "persons desirous of obtaining the likeness of Major General Andrew Jackson" that he was planning an edition of five hundred to be engraved by the celebrated Philadelphia engraver David Edwin, after a likeness on view at his Chartres Street studio.

Based on comparisons with Edwin's engraving, Wheeler's original oil portrait was recently identified at the Historical Society of Pennsylvania. Conservation and cleaning have greatly enhanced the painting's warm colors, which, given the crudity of the likeness, seem to evince Wheeler's only strength as a portraitist. His *Jackson,* although historically significant, is really more of a caricature than a lifelike representation.

Nathan W. Wheeler (circa 1789–1849)
Oil on canvas, 1815
76.2 x 65.4 cm. (30 x 25¾ in.)
The Historical Society of Pennsylvania

General Andrew Jackson Before Judge Hall

Even after his victory at New Orleans on January 8, 1815, Andrew Jackson was still not convinced that the British had given up the fight; and so he decided to maintain martial law throughout the town. Shortly thereafter, rumors spread that a peace treaty ending the War of 1812 had been signed in Ghent. Angry at not having been officially notified, Jackson caused a furor when he attempted to prevent the local newspapers from spreading the rumors.

Affairs continued to worsen. By the end of February, the Louisiana militia considered mutiny if they were not discharged. Next, Creole soldiers, who decided to register with their consul as French citizens, demanded immediate release from their military commitments. Thereupon, Jackson banished them, as well as the consul, from the city. An article in a local French newspaper stated that he had overstepped his bounds, which only enraged Jackson more. The editor was brought before him and forced into revealing the name of the author—Louis Louailler, a member of the legislature. Jackson had him hunted down and thrown into jail. When federal district judge Dominick Augustine Hall intervened, Jackson jailed him for inciting mutiny and then banished him from New Orleans.

Fortunately, on March 13 official word arrived that the peace treaty had been signed, and Jackson promptly ended martial law. Hall now struck back, holding Jackson in contempt of court for refusing to comply with the writ of habeas corpus issued in the Louailler case. Jackson was eventually saddled with a one-thousand-dollar fine for his offense.

Schussele's portrait of Jackson before Judge Hall was commissioned by C. J. Hedenberg, a successful Philadelphia shoe merchant who lived near the artist's studio. Conspicuously centered is the figure of Andrew Jackson. His likeness is a composite taken from unknown portraits. Other prominent figures in the scene, besides Judge Hall, include Jackson's aides-de-camp and counsel, Edward Livingston and Major John Reid. Both men are holding documents of defense and flank their celebrated commander.

Christian Schussele (1824–1879)
Oil on canvas, 1859
108 x 152.4 cm. (42½ x 60 in.)
The Thomas Gilcrease Institute of American History and Art

"See the Conquering Hero Comes"

IN JANUARY 1819 JACKSON WENT TO WASHINGTON TO DEFEND his conduct in the Seminole War of 1818. Jackson had marched an army into Spanish-held West Florida to quell Indian uprisings along the Georgia border and had driven off the Spanish. Both houses of Congress were beginning to question the legality of this episode, and to talk of censuring Jackson. The House Committee on Military Affairs, assigned to investigate the matter, determined that Jackson should be rebuked for ordering the executions of two British subjects, Robert Ambrister and Alexander Arbuthnot, even though they had been found guilty by a military court of aiding the Indians. The House committee also disapproved of Jackson's unauthorized seizures of St. Marks and Pensacola. Jackson had correctly guessed President James Monroe's secret desire to acquire Florida, but his reckless bayonet diplomacy severely embarrassed the administration and invited ugly confrontations with both Spain and England.

As Congress prepared for a major debate, Jackson grew restless in Nashville, wondering whether he should venture to Washington in his own defense. Some of his friends advised him to do so, while others feared that he would lose his equanimity and only harm his cause. Never one to sit idle and let others decide his fate, in the end Jackson hastened to the capital city.

On February 8 the House of Representatives voted to vindicate Jackson. With his hero's image hardly scratched, the general then embarked upon a three-week triumphal tour of the Northeast's major cities. Until this time, a satisfactory likeness of Jackson had not been executed. But now he would be amidst some of the country's best portraitists, who would take advantage of the occasion.

Andrew Jackson
by Charles Willson Peale

No one in Washington was more excited about Jackson's expected arrival there in late January 1819 than Charles Willson Peale. Then in the twilight of his splendid and varied career, Peale had been, at one time or another, a saddler, artist, soldier, and naturalist. His reputation, however, rested on his portrait painting. In mid-November he had journeyed to Washington, intending to take the likenesses of eminent personages for placement in his own Philadelphia museum.

While Congress was conducting its investigation of Jackson, Peale grew restless, waiting for the general to arrive. Although Jackson avoided most social gatherings, preferring instead to meet with his cohorts to plan his counter-offensive, he did consent to let Peale paint his portrait. On at least three occasions he visited the artist's rented studio.

During one sitting, Peale felt disposed to give Jackson "a piece of advice," warning him against fighting a duel. When Jackson asked how in some cases it could be avoided, Peale advised him to rise above ignominy. If Jackson winced at this—sitting with bullets lodged in his chest and shoulder, both the result of personal feuds—Peale never noticed. Only afterward did he learn of Jackson's exploits on the field of honor.

Charles Willson Peale (1741–1827)
Oil on canvas, 1819
71.1 x 56.8 cm. (28 x 22⅜ in.)
The Masonic Library and Museum of
Pennsylvania

Andrew Jackson
by Thomas Sully

After Jackson's arrival in Philadelphia in 1819, one of the many honors bestowed upon him was an invitation from the Association of American Artists to sit for a portrait by Thomas Sully. At thirty-five, Sully was one of America's premier painters. On February 17, with Jackson posed in front of him, Sully began to roughly sketch a study portrait, which he finished the following week.

Between March 26 and April 15, Sully painted this three-quarter-length portrait of Jackson for the association. It was their intention to have the painting engraved by James B. Longacre and sold as a print. Throughout his career Sully executed nearly a dozen portraits of Jackson; yet only this 1819 likeness is known to have been based on a life sitting. Exhibited that year at the Pennsylvania Academy of the Fine Arts, the painting is initialed and dated on the horse's bridle, just over Jackson's right shoulder.

Thomas Sully (1783–1872)
Oil on canvas, 1819
118.1 x 93.9 cm. (46½ x 37 in.)
New York State Office of Parks, Recreation and Historic Preservation, Clermont State Historic Site

Andrew Jackson
by Samuel Lovett Waldo

Of the portraits painted of Jackson during his visit to New York in 1819, the likeness executed by Samuel Lovett Waldo was perhaps the most lifelike in its spontaneity. Jackson appears to have just turned his head, as if distracted in a crowd. His eyes, bright and alert, rivet the viewer. In this replica, copied from the original study, Waldo also hints at Jackson's physical decline on the eve of his fifty-second birthday. This is especially evident around the mouth; Jackson was beginning to lose his teeth one by one.

Samuel Lovett Waldo (1783–1861)
Oil on canvas, circa 1819
84.8 x 67.3 cm. (33⅜ x 26½ in.)
Historic New Orleans Collection; Museum/
Research Center, Acc. No. 1979.112

Andrew Jackson
by John Wesley Jarvis

This portrait was probably painted shortly after Jackson's stay in New York in February 1819. If a flippant account in the *New York Evening Post* can be believed, Jackson did sit for John Wesley Jarvis, one of the city's foremost portraitists. Joseph Rodman Drake, a satirical rhymer, published several accounts of Jackson's itinerary, and on March 11 he quipped:

> *The board is met—the names are read;*
> *Elate of heart the glad committee*
> *Declare the mighty man has said*
> *He'll 'take the freedom of the city.'*
> *He thanks the council and the mayor,*
> *Presents 'em all his humble service;*
> *And thinks he's time enough to spare*
> *To sit an hour or so with Jarvis.*

The following month, Samuel Swartwout, one of Jackson's political cronies in New York, penned the following to the general: *I have just been to see Jarvis' portrait of you. It is inimitable. He has already made 5 copies for different gentlemen. . . . My picture of you, is to be a three quarter full size. Jarvis has a full length for himself. I have not seen Vanderlyne's but understand it is uncommonly fine.*

Swartwout disclosed more information about Jarvis's portraits of Jackson than all other contemporary sources combined. Unfortunately, the present whereabouts of these paintings remains a mystery. Only this three-quarter-length portrait fits Swartwout's description.

John Wesley Jarvis (1780–1840)
Oil on canvas, 1819
123.2 x 91.4 cm. (48½ x 36 in.)
The Metropolitan Museum of Art; Harris Brisbane Dick Fund, 1964

Andrew Jackson
by John Vanderlyn

One of New York City's acclaimed artists, John Vanderlyn was selected by the Common Council to paint a full-length, life-size portrait of Jackson for display in New York City Hall. Vanderlyn executed a study of Jackson's head during the general's visit but was not satisfied with it. He wrestled with this five-hundred-dollar commission for more than a year. Finally, in September 1820, he completed his giant canvas depicting Jackson in full uniform, directing the action on the battlefield at New Orleans. This portrait still hangs in City Hall.

Except for a faithful engraving made from it by Asher B. Durand, Vanderlyn's 1819 likeness is best known through dozens of reproductions based on this head-and-shoulders portrait. This porcelain vase, made in France in about 1825–1830, attests to the popularity of Andrew Jackson abroad.

John Vanderlyn (1755–1852)
Oil on canvas, circa 1819
68.6 x 57.2 cm. (27 x 22½ in.)
City Hall Collection, Charleston, South Carolina

After John Vanderlyn
Porcelain vase, circa 1825–1830
32.5 cm. (12¹³⁄₁₆ in.)
The White House Collection

Andrew Jackson
by Rembrandt Peale

As a special memento of Jackson's visit to Baltimore in 1819, the City Council invited him to have his likeness painted by Rembrandt Peale. Peale, whose artistic interests had been nurtured in his youth by his remarkable father, Charles Willson Peale, opened his own museum in a newly erected three-story brick building on North Holliday Street in 1814. Jackson sat for Peale three times during his three-day visit. The morning after his departure for Washington, a notice appeared in the local newspaper announcing that Peale's portrait of the general would be placed on display in the museum for that evening only. That canvas was only a study portrait and may not yet have been completed. Several days later, Peale's daughter, Rosalba, wrote to a Philadelphia relative with news that her father had just painted an excellent likeness of Jackson and was making a copy for the City Hall. The portrait shown here is now a part of the collection of the Peale Museum.

Rembrandt Peale (1778–1860)
Oil on canvas, 1819
95.3 x 77.5 cm. (37½ x 30½ in.)
Baltimore City Life Museums

CHAPTER 5

The Presidential Chair

BEGINNING IN THE EARLY 1820s, THE PERCEPTION OF ANDREW Jackson progressively changed from that of a military hero to that of a presidential front-runner. George Washington had been the first to experience this transformation; Jackson would be the next. Jackson was driven by a sense of duty to his country, and in the expanding realm of national affairs, the opportunities to serve seemed endless. Already Jackson had answered his nation's call in the Creek War of 1813–1814, at New Orleans in 1814–1815, and in the Seminole Campaign of 1818. Three years later, he returned to Florida, just newly acquired from Spain, as territorial governor. He held this presidential appointment for only a few months, however. In the fall of 1821 Jackson arrived home in Tennessee, exhausted and nearly broken in health, but satisfied in having once again served his government.

For all his patriotism, Jackson did not promote himself for the presidency. Because it was then already ritual in the fledgling arena of republican politics for regional party caucuses to nominate heads of state, Jackson would not even let it appear to the American electorate that he approved of the politicking of his cronies and friends. In his letters and business dealings, Jackson assumed the image of a gentleman farmer, content in retirement.

Notwithstanding some loopholes in the portrait record of the 1820s, the extant likenesses reflect the changes in Jackson's physical appearance and political image as he marched off the battlefield and into the presidential mansion. The most obvious change was in his dress. With one or two exceptions, artists preferred depicting Jackson in traditional civilian attire—black coat and white jabot—rather than in a general's uniform. This squirely image was consistent with his new station in life. Another significant change was in Jackson's hair, which no longer looked as if he had just bivouacked on the windswept Mississippi delta. Now he began keeping it brushed back from his high forehead in a tidier fashion. This enhanced his Washington image both as United States senator, from 1823 to 1825, and later as President. Moreover, his pompadour would become his most distinctive feature.

Andrew Jackson
by John Vanderlyn

Jackson's election to the Senate, which brought him to Washington in the winter of 1823–1824, was part of his strategy to gain the presidency. Although his enormous popularity in Tennessee had inspired the Tennessee legislature to nominate him for that office two years earlier, he was strongly opposed by Colonel John Williams, a candidate for reelection to the United States Senate. Jackson ran against Williams and defeated him, eliminating an important obstacle to his ambition.

In January, Jackson consented to sit for this portrait by John Vanderlyn. Vanderlyn had completed a full-length of him four years earlier, commissioned by the Common Council of New York. This time the city of Charleston, South Carolina, was commissioning a full-length portrait for its City Hall. Vanderlyn painted the head in Washington, but returned to his studio in New York to complete the torso. Recognizing a suitable model in the figure of his friend John James Audubon, Vanderlyn coaxed the noted naturalistic painter to pose.

Vanderlyn's Charleston portrait depicts Jackson in transition. The head reveals the new senator from Tennessee, recently arrived in Washington, rejuvenated in health, confident in his legislative capacity, and full of anticipation for the future. The figure, on the other hand, garbed in the smart dress blues of a major general, places him in the more familiar context of hero of New Orleans. Both depictions were accurate. Although Jackson was now a serious candidate for the presidency, his credentials had United States Army stamped all over them.

John Vanderlyn (1775–1852)
Oil on canvas, 1824
248.9 x 158.8 cm. (98 x 62½ in.)
City Hall Collection, Charleston, South
Carolina

Andrew Jackson
by Robert Street

In the early spring of 1824, Robert Street,
a young portraitist from Philadelphia,
was painting in Washington. Little is
known of Street, except that he had
painted mostly family portraits and
religious, historical, and landscape
paintings, and exhibited more than two
hundred of these in 1840 at the Artist's
Fund Hall in Philadelphia. Although
Washington was bustling with
personalities who were making history at
the time of Street's visit—men like
Monroe, Clay, Calhoun, Webster, and
Adams—it seems that only Jackson
caught the artist's attention.

Why just Old Hickory? Was he the only
public servant in whom Street was
interested; or perhaps was he the only
sitter available? These questions make his
oil portrait of Jackson even more
intriguing. For the first time in a
documented canvas, signed "R. Street,
1824," Jackson appears in civilian attire.
The image is not handsome, but it is
dignified. In the tired eyes and in the
lines of his face, Jackson shows his age
more than in any previous portrait.
Although the presidency was still four
years off, Old Hickory bears more the
look of a successful candidate than a
seasoned general.

Robert Street (1796–1865)
Oil on canvas, 1824
92.1 x 76.2 cm. (36¼ x 30 in.)
Sedalia Public Library

William H. Crawford

In the opinion of Andrew Jackson, presidential contender William H. Crawford (1772–1834) of Georgia was a fitting representative of James Monroe's palsied administration, ridden with scandal and fraud. Although Crawford, as secretary of the treasury, was personally able to dodge charges of bribery and graft, his ambition for the presidency was enough to invite public inquiry into his possible abuse of power to further his own political ends. Jackson's suspicion that there was a cabal to put Crawford in the White House was all but confirmed in 1824 by a congressional caucus that selected him as the preferred candidate. What made the choice of Crawford doubly startling was the fact that he had suffered, in the summer of 1823, a severe, debilitating stroke. New York portraitist John Wesley Jarvis painted this likeness of Crawford the winter before that illness—a large man of commanding presence, who was then still in vigorous health.

John Wesley Jarvis (1780–1840)
Oil on canvas, 1823
76.8 x 64.1 cm. (30¼ x 25¼ in.)
Pennsylvania Academy of the Fine Arts;
gift of Charles Roberts

Henry Clay

Andrew Jackson saw in Henry Clay
(1777–1852) a political charlatan, a viper-
tongued, vote-swapping politician so full
of ambition that he would compromise
the tenets of republican democracy to
further his own selfish ends. Clay was in
fact a consummate politician and a grand
worker of the legislative process of
compromise. Moreover, he was a
nationalist of extraordinary vision. His
"American System"—a government-
backed formula for spurring economic
growth through protective tariffs,
internal improvements, and centralized
banking—left conservative thinkers like
Jackson shaking their heads in disbelief.

Their animosity dated back to 1819
when Clay, as Speaker of the House of
Representatives, denounced Jackson for
his unauthorized invasion of Spanish
West Florida the previous year. In 1825
Clay cast the deciding vote in the House,
assuring John Quincy Adams of the
presidency. When Adams nominated
Clay to the position of secretary of state,
then a stepping-stone to the presidency,
Jackson, the most popular of the leading
candidates, charged that a corrupt bargain had been struck. Four years later, on
the strength of his military career, the
nation elected Jackson President. Although neither man ever understood the
other, the country was better served by
the disparate qualities that each brought
to the democratic process.

George P. A. Healy (1813–1894)
Oil on canvas, circa 1845
76.2 x 63.5 cm. (30 x 25 in.)
National Portrait Gallery, Smithsonian
Institution; transfer from the National
Gallery of Art, gift of Andrew W. Mellon,
1942

John Quincy Adams

Nicknamed Old Man Eloquent, John Quincy Adams of Massachusetts (1767–1848) seemed eminently qualified to become President: he was a man of culture and of extensive learning; he had gained valuable experience as a diplomat and statesman in the administrations of Madison and Monroe; and he had the example of his own father. Adams, however, lacked the one quality necessary for success as chief of state—a hold on the people. His utopian visions of an America steeped in the arts and advanced sciences were lost on a nation of farmers and tradesmen.

In June 1833, diarist Philip Hone wrote, *Poor Adams used to visit New York during his presidency. The papers, to be sure, announced his arrival; but he was welcomed by no shouts, no crowds thronged around his portals, no huzzas rent the air when he made his appearance, and yet posterity, more just than ourselves, will acknowledge him to have been in all the qualifications which constitute his fitness to fill the office of a ruler of this great republic, twenty times superior to Jackson. He wanted tact. He gave the toast of* Ebony and Topaz, *the ungracious offspring of a mind loaded with study and unskillful in adaptation. And the other, in a moment when we were all anxious to save the country . . . and when we doubted what his course would be, gave in a happy moment his toast, "The Union—it must be preserved." It made a difference of five hundred thousand votes. Adams is the wisest man, the best scholar, the most accomplished statesman; but Jackson has most tact. So huzza for Jackson!*

Chester Harding (1792–1866)
Oil on canvas, 1827–1828
76.2 x 66 cm. (30 x 26 in.)
Redwood Library and Athenaeum

Andrew Jackson
by Aaron Corwine

In late March 1825 Senator Andrew
Jackson, defeated in his bid for the
presidency, left Washington and made
the long journey home to the Hermitage.
Only days before, he had personally
extended his congratulations to the
nation's sixth President, John Quincy
Adams. Jackson had won a plurality of
votes in the election of 1824, but it was
not enough to assure him of victory, and
he felt cheated by what he considered to
have been a collapse in the democratic
process.

Tired, angry, and bitter—such was
Jackson's state of mind on his homeward
trek. His route via the National Road
took him over the Allegheny Mountains
near Cumberland, Maryland, and
westward to the banks of the Ohio River
at Wheeling. On Sunday, March 27, he
and his entourage arrived in Cincinnati.
Sometime during his four-day visit, he sat
for this portrait by Aaron Houghton
Corwine. Only in his early twenties, the
self-taught Corwine was the city's first
portraitist. His candid portrayal of
Jackson, finished in April 1825, was the
finest likeness done to date; today it
ranks among Jackson's best.

Aaron H. Corwine (1802–1830)
Oil on canvas, 1825
69.9 x 55.9 cm. (27½ x 22 in.)
Mr. and Mrs. Jackson P. Ravenscroft

The coffin handbill incident

Few presidential elections have provoked more character assassination than the contest of 1828 between incumbent John Quincy Adams and Old Hickory. Particularly vexing was the coffin handbill published by John Binns, editor of the Philadelphia *Democratic Press*. It alleged that six militiamen, in September 1814, disputed the length of their enlistments, were found guilty of desertion and mutiny, and were later ordered by General Jackson to be executed. Binns circulated several thousand of these disparaging supplements in his daily, triweekly, and weekly editions. The original version, labeled *Monumental Inscriptions!*, depicted six large black coffins, each bearing the name and a brief account of one of the condemned militiamen.

Ultimately the coffin handbill turned against John Binns. On repeated occasions angry mobs threatened to snatch him from his premises and bandy him about town in a coffin. Binns's readership eroded until financial difficulties finally necessitated the discontinuance of his paper. His fate was caricatured in an anonymous cartoon, titled *The Pedlar and His Pack or the Desperate Effort, an Over Balance*, which depicts Binns being overburdened with coffins. The two figures balanced precariously on top are Henry Clay (left) and John Quincy Adams. Clay acknowledges that, in his bid for the presidency, he is sinking like Binns, but he urges Adams to hold on to the presidential chair. Adams replies that he will hang on in spite of the coffin handbills and the "wishes of the people."

Monumental Inscriptions!

Broadside, 1828
Louisiana State Museum

The Pedlar and His Pack or the Desperate Effort, an Over Balance

Unidentified artist
Hand-colored engraving, 1828
41.3 x 48.3 cm. (16¼ x 19 in.) framed
Tennessee State Museum

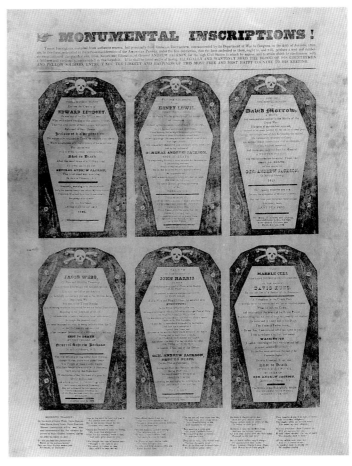

Richard III

Such was the talent of Philadelphia caricaturist David Claypoole Johnston that print and book dealers shunned his satiric sketches because they feared libel suits. This composite portrait of Jackson, titled *Richard III*, illustrated just how venomous his work could be. In this single sketch, probably published in 1828, Johnston derides Jackson's entire military career. Naked corpses compose the general's face; six more bodies form the braid of his right epaulet, and two additional ones constitute his left. These are, no doubt, allusions to the executions of the six militiamen and to Ambrister and Arbuthnot. The two figures holding a white sheet labeled "Habeas corpus" allude to Jackson's arrest of Louis Louailler in New Orleans in 1815 for a petty violation of martial law; when Judge Dominick A. Hall issued a writ of habeas corpus, Jackson jailed him too.

Johnston plumbed the depths of his imagination in this work; cannons become coat collars, and a tent becomes a hat, the plume of which is a gun barrel billowing smoke. He may have drawn inspiration from an 1813 German caricature of Napoleon, whose visage was also composed of carcasses. A veteran of the stage, Johnston tapped Shakespeare for the title, *Richard III*, and for a line from act 5, scene 3: "Methought the souls of all that I had murder'd, came to my tent."

David Claypoole Johnston (1799–1865)
Engraving, circa 1828
16.8 x 11.4 cm. (6⅝ x 4½ in.)
The New-York Historical Society

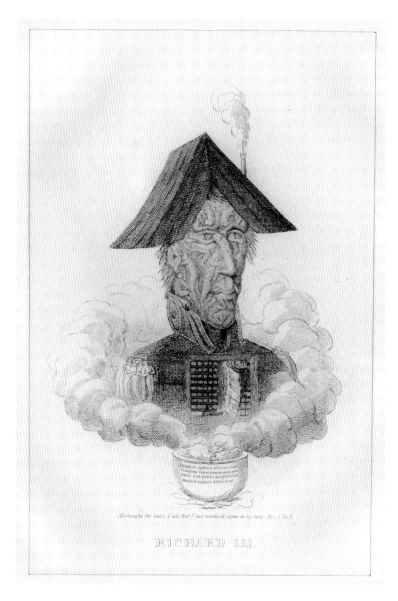

Jackson a Negro Trader

Typical of the defamatory literature
generated by the presidential campaign
of 1828 was this broadside labeling
Jackson a "Negro Trader." Jackson, a
large landowner, did buy and sell slaves
as his planting interests dictated. By the
time he became President in 1829, he
was keeping ninety-five slaves at the
Hermitage, his estate outside of Nashville. Jackson, however, never made a
business of trading in slaves as this
broadside charges.

Broadside, 1828
Rare Book and Special Collections Division,
Library of Congress

Jackson and a Standing Army

This anti-Jackson broadside casts him as a military tyrant, who, if elected President, would bring ruin upon the country.

Broadside, 1828
Tennessee Historical Society

Jackson Men, Look Out for the Spurious Ticket

This pro-Jackson broadside warns voters to be wary of political trickery when casting their ballots.

Broadside, circa 1824 or 1828
Tennessee Historical Society

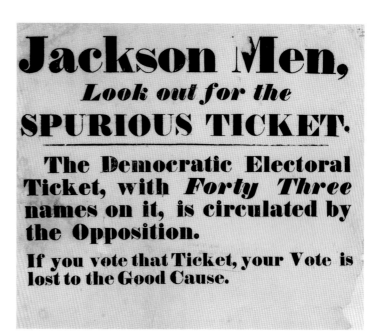

**Tortoiseshell comb, circa 1828,
with image of Andrew Jackson,
after Joseph Wood**

National Museum of American History,
Smithsonian Institution; Mrs. Moncure
Burke Collection

Rachel Jackson

On December 22, 1828, in the midst of making preparations to become first lady, Rachel Jackson died suddenly from what her doctors diagnosed as heart failure, complicated by a cold. Andrew, however, always held his political enemies responsible, for indeed their slanders and forthright accusations of adultery and bigamy had severely depressed Rachel and noticeably weakened her health. This reaction to her husband's election to the presidency reflected her disillusionment with politics. "I assure you," she once said, "I had rather be a doorkeeper in the house of God than to live in that palace at Washington."

This portrait of Rachel, painted by Ralph E. W. Earl in about 1827, was considered by the artist to have been the best representation from life. From it, and at Jackson's request, Earl made at least one romanticized copy.

Ralph E. W. Earl (circa 1788–1838)
Oil on canvas, circa 1827
73.7 x 60.9 cm. (29 x 24 in.)
The Hermitage: Home of President Andrew Jackson

CHAPTER 6

President Jackson

ANDREW JACKSON WON THE PRESIDENTIAL CONTEST OF 1828, THIS
time decisively beating the incumbent, John Quincy Adams. For the first time
in America's history, a westerner, a man of unusually humble beginnings and
simple tastes, had been elected President of the United States. Although his
only real distinction was as the hero of New Orleans—scarcely a qualification
for running the government—Jackson transformed the office of the presidency into one of dynamic leadership and national initiative. No longer would
the chief executive be merely an armchair overseer of Congress and the nation
at large. Moreover, his sweeping reform program extolled the principles of
democratic government by the will of the people. These tenets of Jacksonian
democracy are just as relevant today.

The portrait record of Jackson as President is a rich one. Numerous
painters, sculptors, and sketch artists visited the White House with a single
goal. Ralph E. W. Earl is especially noteworthy. Having made Jackson's
acquaintance in 1817, Earl became a devoted friend and confidant. During
Jackson's eight years in office, Earl lived in the executive mansion and painted
more than two dozen portraits of him. Ironically for a chief of state who
ignored the advancement of the arts in America, Jackson had in Earl what
many considered a court painter.

Significant, too, were the dozens of political cartoons. Jackson's presidency
had much to do with their sudden proliferation in the 1830s. First, his election
roughly coincided with the beginning of commercial lithography in America,
the inexpensive medium in which most cartoons were produced. Second,
President Jackson provided graphic jesters with an unusually colorful and
controversial figure to lampoon. In addition to their value as biased political
commentary, the cartoons collectively form a unique and lifelike portrait of
the nation's seventh President.

Jackson as the Great Father

Nothing stirred Jackson's blood quite like talk of Indians. In early December of 1829, in his first annual message to Congress, Jackson jolted the legislature with a proposal to move them to un-occupied lands west of the Mississippi. The idea was not new. Shared by such Presidents as Washington and Jefferson, it originated as an alternative to the failed dream of Anglicizing America's natives.

In the spring of 1830, after heated debate in both houses of Congress, the Indian Removal Bill passed by narrow margins. Signed by Jackson into law on May 28, this bill proved to be the only significant legislative accomplishment of his first term. Bold and rash, the measure was typically Jacksonian. At that time the majority of Americans believed that removal was good for the Indian and right for the nation. Yet this brand of democracy by decree, involving untold numbers of individuals and countless dollars, would come to be viewed as a national disgrace.

This anonymous cartoon, depicting Jackson as the Great Father, satirizes his compassion for the Indians, which was anything but embracing.

Unidentified artist
Lithograph, not dated
31.8 x 23.3 cm. (12½ x 9³/₁₆ in.)
William L. Clements Library, University of Michigan, Ann Arbor

Andrew Jackson peace medal with beadwork necklace and eagle claw ornament

Since George Washington's administration, it had been the government's practice to mint and issue Indian peace medals. These tokens of friendship were bestowed upon chiefs and other important tribesmen on such special occasions as the signing of treaties, visits to Washington by tribal delegations, and official government tours through Indian territories. By 1829 the medals had become so esteemed by the Indians that it was difficult to conduct meaningful business without them. The Indians wore the medals around their necks and valued them as badges of power and prestige.

Moritz Fürst (born 1782)
Silver, circa 1832
7.6 cm. (3 in.) diameter
National Museum of the American Indian,
Smithsonian Institution

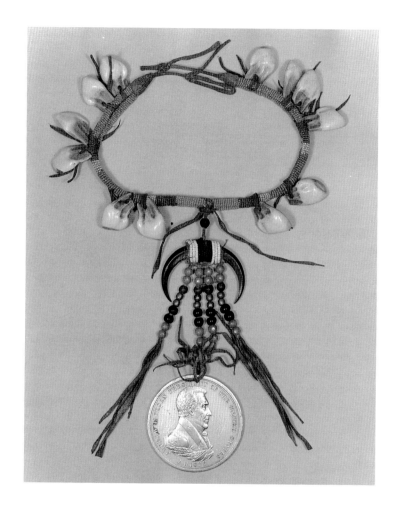

President Jackson in 1830

Born in Windham County, Connecticut, in 1800, Francis Alexander did not fully discover his talent for painting until early in his twenties. Initially aspiring only to be a sign painter, he made two trips to New York City, where he received professional instruction, and thus discovered portraiture. He returned home, plied his newfound skills on the local populace, and became widely known for his charmingly accurate likenesses.

In Washington during the winter of 1830, Alexander was just entering upon the most productive phase of his career. His portrait of Andrew Jackson has a straightforward simplicity. A description of Jackson by James Stuart, a Scotsman touring the United States at that time, corroborated this likeness. Jackson, wrote Stuart, *has very little the appearance or gait of a soldier. . . . He is extremely spare in his habit of body, at first sight not altogether unlike Shakespeare's starved apothecary, but he is not an ungenteel man in manner and appearance; and there are marks of good humor, as well as of decision of character, in his countenance.*

Francis Alexander (1800–1880)
Oil on panel, 1830
75.6 x 62.9 cm. (29¾ x 24¾ in.)
Private collection

Martin Van Buren

In the politically charged era of Jacksonian America, a time when great and talented men like Webster, Clay, and Calhoun were avidly seeking the presidency to no avail, Martin Van Buren (1782–1862) was looked upon by his adversaries as a wolf in sheepskin. Nicknamed the Little Magician, Van Buren did, in fact, cloak his ambitions under a mantle of charm, patience, and self-control. An accomplished lawyer, he was governor of New York before joining Jackson's administration as secretary of state and later as Vice President. Jackson came to rely heavily on his sound judgment and political instincts in formulating policies on such volatile issues as nullification and rechartering the Bank of the United States. Van Buren, for his part, kept his political views routinely in Jackson's shadow. Lacking his mentor's hero's hold on the people, Van Buren understood the practicality of nodding and even prattling to the common man. A literary jester once compared his politics to an amorphous piece of cloth: "No one could tell whether it was made of cotton or flax, hemp or wool—twilled or plain, striped or checker'd—but a little of all on 'em."

Van Buren's political prowess and loyalty to Jackson paid off in the presidential contest of 1836. As Jackson's hand-picked successor, he won the presidency.

Francis Alexander (1800–1880)
Oil on panel, circa 1830–1840
76.4 x 61.1 cm. (30⅟₁₆ x 24⅟₁₆ in.)
The White House Collection

Peggy Eaton

Beguiling and pretty, Margaret (Peggy) Eaton (1799–1879), the wife of Secretary of War John Henry Eaton, indirectly caused much rancor during Jackson's first administration. The two had met in about 1818, when Eaton, a new senator from Tennessee, took up lodgings in the Washington boardinghouse run by Peggy's father, William O'Neale. She was then the wife of John B. Timberlake, a navy purser who died ten years later amid rumors of malfeasance and suicide. Eaton's subsequent courtship of Peggy seemed only to confirm the talk of his prior affection for her.

Andrew Jackson, himself a former boarder at the O'Neales' during his own brief Senate career, was an old friend of Eaton and an admirer of Peggy. To put an end to gossip, he encouraged their marriage, which occurred on January 1, 1829. Nevertheless, persistent rumors followed both Jackson and Eaton into office and kept Washington society buzzing for the next two years. Affairs degenerated to the point at which the wives and daughters of several cabinet members refused to attend social gatherings and state dinners to which Mrs. Eaton had been invited. Jackson, incensed by the acrimonious rumors and slights, defended Peggy's honor as if it were that of his own deceased wife.

Henry Inman (1801–1846)
Oil on canvas, not dated
74.9 x 63.5 cm. (29½ x 25 in.)
The Hermitage: Home of President Andrew Jackson

Study sketch of Jackson for political cartoons

Political caricaturist Edward Williams Clay of Philadelphia was never among Jackson's ardent supporters. Unfortunately for the President, this graphic jester proved to be the most prolific cartoonist of the 1830s and 1840s.

Trained in the law, Clay had a deft mind and obviously appreciated the nuances of political satire. Much of his success as a caricaturist stemmed from his skill as a portraitist—as seen in this original sketch of Jackson's profile. Jackson's features—pursed mouth, straight nose, bushy eyebrows, lined forehead, bristling locks, and even his adjustable folding spectacles—have been faithfully replicated. Clay used this view in many of his cartoons, which hints that it was his principal model.

Edward Williams Clay (1799–1857)
Pencil on paper, 1831
20.3 x 8.3 cm. (8 x 3¼ in.)
National Portrait Gallery, Smithsonian Institution; gift of J. William Middendorf II

The Rats leaving a Falling House

In mid-April of 1831, Jackson's cabinet resigned. A festering rivalry between Secretary of State Van Buren and Vice President Calhoun, which had divided the Democratic party, brought on much of this exodus. Secretary of War Eaton, whose wife Peggy had caused much discord, also resigned.

This cartoon, hastily composed by Edward Williams Clay, broke the news to a completely astounded public. Clay depicts the government in collapse. Scampering away from the perplexed and forlorn President are four rats with recognizable human heads—John Eaton, John Branch (secretary of the navy), Martin Van Buren, and Samuel D. Ingham (secretary of the treasury). Jackson's foot on Van Buren's tail indicates his wish to retain him temporarily.

The Rats, although it shed no real light on the inner workings of the administration, was both effective and widely published. John Quincy Adams recorded that two thousand copies were sold on April 25 in Philadelphia and that ten thousand more would be disposed of within a fortnight. Van Buren's son, asked when his father would be returning to New York, replied, "When the President takes off his foot."

This annotated copy of *The Rats* originally belonged to Samuel Breck, a prominent Philadelphian and diarist of the Jacksonian era.

Edward Williams Clay (1799–1857)
Lithograph, 1831
26.4 x 19.7 cm. (10⅜ x 7¾ in.)
The Library Company of Philadelphia

The Rats leaving a Falling House.

King Andrew the First

Edward Williams Clay dramatized Jackson's apparent sovereignty in a popular broadside, *King Andrew the First, "Born to Command,"* published in about 1834. The President is bedecked in regal splendor—"A King," states the artist, "who, possessing as much power as his Gracious Brother William IV, makes worse use of it." In this cartoon, Jackson literally tramples on the Constitution, internal improvements, and the Bank of the United States. He exercised his veto power more than all of his predecessors combined, and was the first President to use the pocket veto. Such power so amply wielded troubled many of his critics. As Supreme Court Justice Joseph Story observed, "Though we live under the form of a republic we are in fact under the absolute rule of a single man."

Edward Williams Clay (1799–1857)
Lithograph, circa 1834
70.5 x 29.2 cm. (27¾ x 11¾ in.)
Tennessee Historical Society

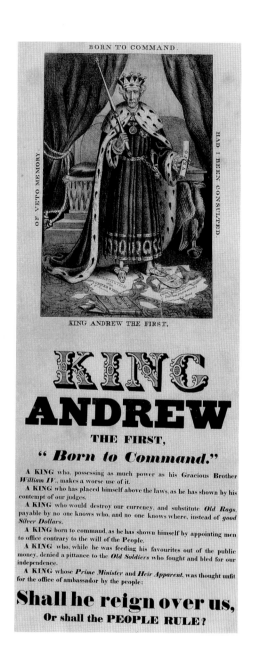

Amos Kendall

Amos Kendall (1789–1869) served Jackson's administration as fourth auditor of the treasury and later as postmaster general. Distinguishing himself as an administrator, Kendall routed corruption, thereby fulfilling one of the President's campaign pledges. Moreover, he was a member of the "Kitchen Cabinet," that influential bevy of advisers upon which Jackson relied almost exclusively.

A New Englander by birth, Kendall migrated to Frankfort, Kentucky, as a young man, where he became editor of the *Argus of Western America*. That paper's support for Jackson in the 1828 election helped to carry the state for him. For Kendall, it proved to be his ticket to Washington. His perspicuity instilled in the administration an intellectual dimension that otherwise would have been lacking.

Prematurely white-haired and sallow complexioned, Kendall suffered from chronically poor health, which kept him out of public view. Still, critics of the administration, in the words of one source, saw Kendall as "the President's *thinking* machine, and his *writing* machine—ay, and his *lying* machine! . . . He was chief overseer, chief reporter, amanuensis, scribe, accountant general, man of all work—nothing was well done without the aid of his diabolical genius."

Charles Fenderich (1805–1887)
Lithograph, 1837
27.6 x 26 cm. (10⅞ x 10¼ in.)
National Portrait Gallery, Smithsonian Institution; transfer from the Library of Congress, Prints and Photographs Division

Amos Kendall
POSTMASTER GENERAL

Francis Preston Blair

Francis P. Blair (1791–1876) epitomized the cabal of advisers to the President known as the Kitchen Cabinet—they allegedly slipped in and out of Jackson's second-floor office via the kitchen. Blair, however, in addition to being a confidant, was the principal spokesman of the administration. An experienced Kentucky journalist, he had been summoned to Washington in 1830 to establish a daily newspaper that would speak for the rights of the common man. Through his prodigious efforts, the Washington *Globe* became an immediate success. Its lucid columns so won Jackson's confidence that whenever he wanted an issue brought before the public, he would say, "Give it to Blair." Seemingly with no reservations, the *Globe* defended the President's every action.

Jackson also had a staunch friend in Blair, a balding, emaciated-looking man of considerable charm and generosity. In 1842, when debt brought Old Hickory to the brink of ruin, Blair stepped forth with a sizeable loan. Such was Jackson's trust in his friend from Silver Spring, Maryland, that before his death he left his "papers and reputation" in Blair's keeping.

Thomas Sully (1783–1872)
Oil on canvas, 1845
74.9 x 62.9 cm. (29½ x 24¾ in.)
Blair House; gift of his great-grandsons
Colonel E. Brooke Lee and P. Blair Lee

A Globe to *Live On!*

This cartoon lampoons the business
partnership of Francis P. Blair (left) and
Amos Kendall, and their efforts to make
the Washington *Globe*, the administration's newspaper, a financial success.
Kendall and Blair, both experienced
journalists, had been friends in Kentucky,
where Blair had contributed editorials to
Kendall's Jacksonian newspaper, *Argus of
Western America*. In 1830, largely at Kendall's urging, Blair moved to Washington
to establish the *Globe*. The two men made
an arrangement whereby Kendall would
write for the paper on a part-time basis,
thus allowing him to perform his new
duties as fourth auditor of the treasury.
Kendall's remuneration, however, would
be linked to subscription sales. Allegedly,
Blair sent papers to every federal
officeholder whose salary exceeded a
thousand dollars. At the end of the year
he would forward a bill, which loyal
Jackson men paid promptly so as not to
jeopardize their job security.

In this cartoon, Blair states Kendall's
worth to the paper: "Amos: You are an
Atlas! and can support the Globe!"
Kendall, holding a subscription list of
officeholders, replies: "Yes! Frank, and
can make the Globe support me."

Napoleon Sarony (1821–1896)
Lithograph, not dated
28.3 x 25.4 cm. (11⅛ x 10 in.)
National Museum of American History,
Smithsonian Institution; Peters Collection

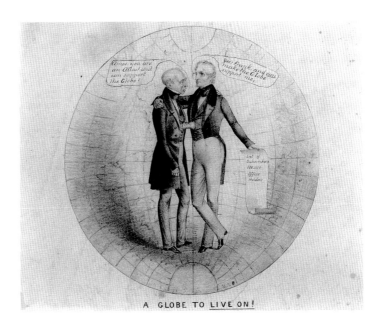

A GLOBE TO LIVE ON!

Office Hunters for the Year 1834

Central to President Jackson's reform program was the need to rid government of inefficiency and corruption. Jackson viewed the federal bureaucracy as an "Augean stable," which had to be thoroughly cleaned. Believing that many officeholders were incompetent or dishonest, he advocated their replacement. "Rotation in office," he postulated, "will perpetuate our liberty." Critics, however, considered this a "spoils system," whereby the politically faithful were rewarded with jobs and patronage. This popular cartoon depicts Jackson as the devil, tantalizing the people with the fruits of victory.

Attributed to James Akin (circa 1773–1846)
Lithograph, 1834
25.1 x 38.7 cm. (9⅞ x 15¼ in.)
National Museum of American History,
Smithsonian Institution; Peters Collection

OFFICE HUNTERS FOR THE YEAR 1834.

John C. Calhoun

John C. Calhoun of South Carolina
(1782–1850) was the foremost southern
politician and statesman of the
Jacksonian era. He entered Congress in
1810 at the politically precocious age of
twenty-eight. Next, he demonstrated
considerable administrative ability as
secretary of war in James Monroe's
cabinet; he became Vice President in
1825. Himself a perennial candidate for
the presidency in the 1820s and 1830s,
Calhoun put aside his own ambitions in
the election of 1828 to support the
favored Jackson. For this sacrifice,
Calhoun was allowed to rest his own
presidential aspirations on the next
election. Jockeying with him was Martin
Van Buren, and their rivalry soon caused
a rift in the cabinet. In part because of
the Eaton scandal, Jackson shifted his
support to the gracious and politically
cunning Van Buren. In February 1831,
Jackson read Calhoun out of the
Democratic party for his disloyalty, and
the following year Calhoun resigned the
vice presidency.

Calhoun's theory of nullification was
enough in itself to have alienated
Jackson. His "South Carolina Exposition"
advanced the doctrine of states' rights,
specifically a state's right to nullify
federal laws that it deemed unconstitutional. South Carolina, in adopting
an Ordinance of Nullification in 1832,
declared the protective tariff acts of 1828
and 1832 "oppressive, unconstitutional,
null and void and not binding on the
people." Jackson held Calhoun
principally responsible for this agitation,
which he was fully prepared to squelch by
force.

William James Hubard (1807–1862)
Oil on panel, circa 1832
49.5 x 37.1 cm. (19½ x 14⅝ in.)
The Corcoran Gallery; museum purchase,
1889

President Jackson's Proclamation addressed to the people of South Carolina, December 10, 1832

President Jackson, a staunch believer in the indissolubility of the Union, disagreed with South Carolina's contention that a state could declare null and void federal laws that it deemed unconstitutional. He argued that nullification would destroy the country; it would be like "a bag of meal with both ends open. Pick it up in the middle or endwise, and it will run out."

In an effort to generate national support for upholding the Union and the Constitution, Jackson issued his famous Proclamation of December 10, 1832, denouncing nullification. Specifically, he was addressing the people of South Carolina as fair warning that defiance of the law would be regarded as treason. Fortunately, the Compromise Tariff of 1833 defused this crisis. Jackson's Proclamation, however, has since become the definitive argument for the Union as a perpetual entity.

Silk broadside, 1832
National Museum of American History,
Smithsonian Institution; DeWitt Collection

Edward Livingston

It was a tribute to Edward Livingston (1764–1836) that the President turned to him in 1832 to help draft his Proclamation to the people of South Carolina, the most important of all Jackson's state papers. Of an old, distinguished New York family, Livingston was trained in the law and was serving in the United States House of Representatives in 1796 when Jackson entered as a new congressman from Tennessee. A lifelong friendship began, which was renewed in New Orleans in 1814 during Jackson's triumphant campaign against the British.

In the spring of 1831, following the breakup of Jackson's cabinet, Livingston became secretary of state. He resigned in 1833 to become minister to France. On foreign soil he performed his last great service to Jackson and the United States in helping to conclude the French spoliation claims controversy. Upon Livingston's sudden death in May 1836, Jackson extended to his widow "the condolence of a sincere and old friend."

James Barton Longacre (1794–1869)
Sepia watercolor on artist board, circa 1833
26 x 20.5 cm. (10¼ x 8¹⁄₁₆ in.)
National Portrait Gallery, Smithsonian Institution

"Farmer Jackson"

This portrait of President Jackson by his good friend Ralph E. W. Earl depicts him as he looked in 1830. Jackson stands on the grounds of the Hermitage, his plantation outside of Nashville. In his letters, Earl referred to this image as "Farmer Jackson." In 1832 the Pendleton lithography company in Boston published a popular lithograph after Earl's likeness.

Ralph E. W. Earl (circa 1788–1838)
Oil on canvas, circa 1832
74.9 x 62.2 cm. (29½ x 24½ in.)
Private collection

Nicholas Biddle

No single issue better exemplified Jackson's executive resolve than his refusal to renew the charter of the second B:..: of the United States. In his first annual message to Congress in December 1829, Jackson expressed concern about the Bank's constitutionality, about the expediency of the law that had created it, and about the general soundness of paper money in lieu of gold and silver specie. Amidst these rumblings, Nicholas Biddle (1786–1844), the Bank's energetic president, grew uneasy about the future of his financial institution housed in Philadelphia. Intent upon provoking the issue in an election year, and with Henry Clay's urging, Biddle applied to Congress in January 1832 for a new charter four years before the expiration of the existing one. Jackson sensed political maneuvering. Suddenly, defeat of the Bank of the United States became his obsession. He considered it to be a monopoly, inherently established to benefit the privileged classes. Its powers, independent of federal and state regulations, were immense and growing. The Bank was a veritable government in itself, exclaimed the President, *"but I will kill it!"*

On July 10, 1832, Jackson vetoed the Bank Bill. Then he made arrangements for removing the government's funds, depositing them in favored state banks. Biddle struck back by calling in loans, thus causing a mild economic contraction throughout the end of 1833 and into 1834. Upon expiration of the Bank's federal charter in 1836, Biddle successfully sought a state charter. His institution became the Bank of the United States of Pennsylvania and functioned much as it had before.

Henry Inman (1801–1846)
Oil on canvas, 1839
88.9 x 68.6 cm. (35 x 27 in.)
The Historical Society of Pennsylvania

The Downfall of Mother Bank

The Bank war spawned numerous political cartoons. Although two-thirds of the press supported the Bank, caricaturists tended either to side with Jackson or remain ambivalent. Edward Williams Clay, in an about-face from earlier works, actually portrayed the President favorably in *The Downfall of Mother Bank*. In the forefront stands Jackson, holding up an "order for the removal of the public money." Biddle's financial temple topples, as if struck by lightning; the demonic Biddle is shown with Webster and Clay, his two chief congressional proponents. Strewn on the floor are partisan newspapers, dependent on the Bank for loans and patronage. On the far right, Major Jack Downing—a facetious literary character created in about 1830 by Seba Smith, editor of the *Portland Courier*—takes his hat off to Jackson while patting him on the back.

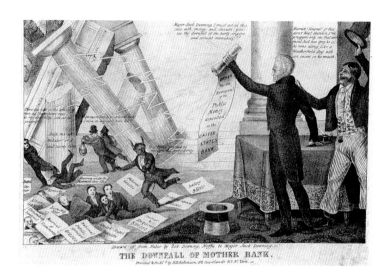

THE DOWNFALL OF MOTHER BANK.

H. R. Robinson (active circa 1831–circa 1851), after Edward Williams Clay
Lithograph, 1833
23.5 x 33.7 cm. (9¼ x 13¼ in.)
American Antiquarian Society

I Take It on My Responsibility

In this anti-Jackson cartoon, Nicholas Biddle (center) is shown leading his cohorts in an attack against the President and his Kitchen Cabinet, who all scurry off for protection among the Greek Revival columns of the United States Bank in Philadelphia.

Unidentified artist
Lithograph, circa 1834
36.8 x 47.3 cm. (14½ x 18⅝ in.)
The Library Company of Philadelphia

Figurehead of Andrew Jackson
carved for the frigate *Constitution*

In the summer of 1834, this figurehead of Andrew Jackson was placed upon the venerable frigate *Constitution* while it was undergoing repairs at the Charleston Navy Yard near Boston. No sooner had it been installed when, under the cover of a stormy night, an intrepid prankster climbed up the ship's bow cable until he had his "arms round the old gentleman's neck," and then proceeded to cut off his head. The next day much of Boston, angered by the President's program of reform, especially his stringent monetary policy, applauded this derring-do.

The following March, Jacksonians were vindicated when a newly carved head by Dodge & Son of New York City was affixed to the frigate. If Bostonians felt any embarrassment about this restoration being completed at another navy yard, New Yorkers could scarcely gloat over the secrecy of the operation, or about the subsequent anchoring of the ship in the lower bay some twenty miles away from the city. "Had the ship been at the wharves of our city," reported the *New York Daily Advertiser,* "or at any place where the populace could have reached her, we very much fear a riot of the most serious consequences would have followed." Such was the unpopularity of Andrew Jackson in the financial centers of the Northeast.

Laban S. Beecher (born circa 1805)
Wood, 1834
274.3 cm. (108 in.)
Museum of the City of New York; gift of the
Seawanhaka Corinthian Yacht Club

Andrew Jackson
by Hiram Powers

American sculptor Hiram Powers, best remembered for such idealistic works as *Eve Tempted* and *Greek Slave,* was also a brilliant portraitist, and his encounter with Andrew Jackson in Washington in 1834 and 1835 was a milestone in his early career. In after years he stated that he had never had a more striking subject than the general. Moreover, Powers held that his bust of Jackson "was the original cause of all my success since."

Powers worked in a vacant room inside the presidential mansion. In approximately three one-hour sessions, Jackson passed the time by smoking his long-stemmed clay pipe and reading the newspapers from his part of Tennessee. As Powers was finishing the bust, Jackson's former ward and secretary, Andrew Jackson Donelson, stopped in to inspect the work. He highly approved, except for the mouth, which he felt had been copied too faithfully, "alleging that the General had lost his teeth, or rather, laid them aside, and that his mouth had fallen in." Powers, though not persuaded, thought best to consult Jackson about this. "Make me as I am," Jackson ordered. "I have no desire to *look* young as long as I *feel* old."

According to one source, *Mr. Powers has succeeded to a charm. He presents the old man precisely as he looks when receiving company in the East Room on a levee night. There is a peculiar position of the head, when listening to the compliments of flatterers, the chin thrown a little forward, the wrinkles all over the face in full play, and the mouth just ready to speak. It is General Jackson to the life.*

Hiram Powers (1805–1873)
Plaster, 1834–1835
72.1 cm. (28⅜ in.)
National Museum of American Art, Smithsonian Institution; museum purchase in memory of Ralph Cross Johnson

The Attempted Assassination, of the President of the United States, January 30, 1835

The attempted assassination of President Jackson on January 30, 1835, produced a lithograph that was just as unique in its news commentary as the actual event was in the national experience. Never before in the forty-year history of the presidency had such a deadly assault been attempted.

The incident occurred after funeral services had been held in the House Chamber for Representative Warren R. Davis of South Carolina. As Jackson was leaving the Capitol rotunda, a young man sprang from the crowd and leveled a pistol at him. The day being exceedingly damp, only the percussion cap exploded, failing to ignite the powder inside the barrel. A shot with a second pistol proved equally harmless. As a presidential escort knocked the assailant to the ground, Old Hickory had to be restrained from thrashing the gunman with his cane. Jackson was then whisked back to the White House, where Vice President Van Buren observed him, moments later, "sitting with one of Major Donelson's children on his lap and conversing with General [Winfield] Scott, himself apparently the least disturbed person in the room." The assailant, Richard Lawrence, an unemployed house painter, was arrested, tried, and found innocent by reason of insanity.

Unidentified artist
Lithograph, 1835
33.9 x 42.9 cm. (13⅜ x 16⅞ in.)
Prints and Photographs Division, Library of Congress

THE ATTEMPTED ASSASSINATION, OF THE PRESIDENT OF UNITED STATES, JAN. 30. 1835.

President Jackson
by Asher B. Durand

When New York engraver Asher B.
Durand journeyed to Washington in
February 1835, it marked a turning point
in his career, first toward painting
portraits, and then painting landscapes
in the mode of the Hudson River School.
Commissioned by Luman Reed, a pros-
perous merchant and benefactor of the
arts, to execute a likeness of Andrew
Jackson, Durand had to wait for ten days
and complained about "having to dance
attendance on 'great men.'" When he
finally got his chance at Jackson, he made
the most of it. The President, he wrote,
"has been part of the time in a pretty
good humor, but some times he gets
his 'dander up' & smokes his pipe
prodigiously."

   Durand was able to obtain only four or
five sittings, but they were enough for
him to capture what one journal
described as "not merely a likeness, but a
facsimile." Indeed, his portrait was about
as close to real life as any two-dimen-
sional work could possibly be. It conjures
up the description left by an unidentified
American who had interviewed Jackson a
few years earlier. *His face is unlike any
other: its prevailing expression is energy. . . .
His eye is of a dangerous fixedness, deep set,
and overhung by bushy gray eyebrows, his
features long, with strong, ridgy lines running
through his cheeks; his forehead a good deal
seamed; and his white hair, stiff and wiry,
brushed obstinately back, and worn quite with
an expression of a* chevaux de frise *of
bayonets. In his mouth there is a redeeming
suavity as he speaks; but the instant his lips
close, a vizor of steel would scarcely look more
impenetrable.*

Asher B. Durand (1796–1886)
Oil on canvas, 1835
81.3 x 66 cm. (32 x 26 in.)
United States Naval Academy Museum

The Old Lion, and the Cock What Won't Fight

Jackson's hard-line rhetoric and uncompromising posture in settling the French spoliation claims for once united the entire nation behind him. The French government was the antagonist this time. The trouble stemmed from its delinquency in paying the first six installments of a twenty-five-million-franc indemnity for depredations against United States shipping interests during the Napoleonic wars. The initial payment was to have been made a year after the treaty's ratification on February 2, 1832, but by September of 1833 the United States had not received a cent. The American minister, Edward Livingston, had had no difficulty in persuading the king and ministers to meet the obligation. The chambers, however, which had to vote its approval, espoused the French public opinion that this claim was exorbitant.

Convinced that a show of force might be required, Jackson ordered the navy to be ready in June 1834. In his annual message to Congress that year, Jackson strongly suggested that if France continued to shirk her duty, the United States should seize enough French property to satisfy the claim. The President's harsh language offended the French ministry, which abruptly recalled its representative from Washington. Soon after, the chambers voted in favor of honoring the treaty, but with the proviso that Jackson first explain his offensive message. The Americans held that since the President's address was intended solely for Congress, the French, in effect, had no right to read over Uncle Sam's shoulder.

Unidentified artist
Hand-colored lithograph, 1835
26 x 33 cm. (10¼ x 13 in.)
Tennessee State Library and Archives

Andrew Jackson and Louis-Philippe

The United States' successful conclusion of the French spoliation claims controversy in 1836 provided Frenchman Pierre Joseph Landry with an appropriately symbolic topic with which to fuse his nationalistic roots and his American sympathies. His wood carving of Andrew Jackson (left) and King Louis-Philippe of France clasping arms around a tree, emblematic of peace, takes no sides. Its simple message is friendship. The carved base, portraying two ships, each sailing toward the other against a distant sun, holds forth the promise for new ties between the two nations. Landry, a veteran of the New Orleans campaign of 1815, allegedly presented his sculpture to Jackson.

Pierre Joseph Landry (1770–1843)
Wood carving, 1836
64.8 cm. (25½ in.)
The Hermitage: Home of President Andrew Jackson

President Jackson in 1836

Ferdinand Pettrich executed this likeness of President Jackson in 1836, during the final year of his administration. Born in Dresden, Germany, in 1798, Pettrich learned the rudiments of carving from his father, the court sculptor to the King of Saxony. As a young man he journeyed to Rome, where he perfected his skills under Bertel Thorwaldsen, the successful Danish-born sculptor. In 1835 Pettrich and his wife sailed for the United States, settling in Philadelphia and then Washington.

Pettrich's few years in the nation's capital were not very productive, and the modeling of portrait busts became both a necessity for existence and an activity to fill his idle hours. His likenesses of Henry Clay, Amos Kendall, Joel Poinsett, and Martin Van Buren all received favorable notice in newspapers. Oddly, no such record has been discovered for the bust of Andrew Jackson. What little evidence survives suggests that Pettrich met the President in early April of 1836. If his primary goal was to seek Jackson's special favor in winning government commissions, Pettrich also took advantage of the opportunity to study the eminent face before him. Judging from the fidelity of the finished likeness, Jackson may have even granted Pettrich several sittings. This bust is one of four replicas.

Ferdinand Pettrich (1798–1872)
Marble, circa 1836
62.2 cm. (24½ in.)
The Historical Society of Pennsylvania

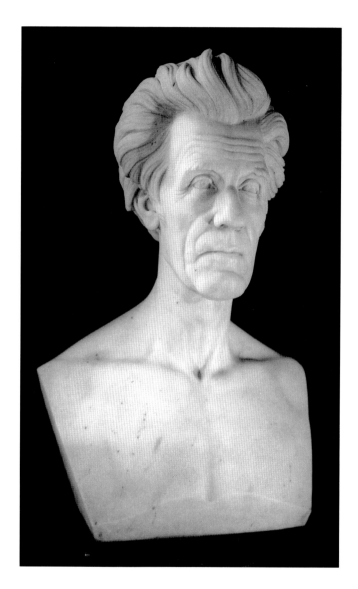

Andrew Jackson before the Hermitage

Sometime during the last months of Jackson's administration, a little-known portrait and genre painter from Philadelphia, named John P. Merrill, executed this unique and charming likeness of the President standing on the front grounds of the Hermitage. Although Jackson did visit his home in the summer of 1836, the inscription on the back of the canvas indicates that Merrill painted the portrait in Washington. The portrait's setting corroborates this because the mansion had burned to the ground two years earlier. The house is depicted as it had looked in 1831. Redesigned and completed in 1836, the new dwelling survives to this day.

Given his relatively robust and idealized appearance in this small portrait, it is uncertain whether Jackson sat for it. The autumn foliage is perhaps symbolic of his age. Although Jackson still occupied the presidential mansion, Merrill's romanticized rendering of him at home very likely portrayed what now lay deepest in the old man's heart.

John P. Merrill (active 1836–1847)
Oil on canvas, 1836
60.3 x 45.1 cm. (23¾ x 17¾ in.)
Mr. and Mrs. John R. Neal

The "National Picture" of President Jackson

Ralph E. W. Earl saved his best portrait of Jackson for last. In December 1836, just a few months before the end of Jackson's administration, Earl was at work upon a full-length, life-size portrait of the President. The last time he had painted a grand canvas was in 1821, when he executed a copy of the hero of New Orleans for that city. In this new work, painted for the city of Washington, Earl depicted Jackson standing on the south portico of the presidential mansion wearing his scarlet-lined military cloak; his familiar white beaver hat lies on a side chair. A reporter for the *Spirit of the Times,* after viewing the painting in the President's "Palace" prior to its removal to City Hall, saw symbolism in the fact that Jackson's back was "*turned upon Congress*," with whom he had quarreled unceasingly for eight years. Another source considered the "autumnal sunset emblematic of his bright and glorious official retirement."

As a true likeness of Andrew Jackson, this was not Earl's best effort. None, however, were as dramatic as this full-size "National Picture." The "perspective is beautiful," wrote the *Times,* and "the conception is admirable." Perhaps the *Boston Statesman* of February 25, 1837, best summed up this image: "It combines the qualities of a portrait, a landscape, and a historical painting." Earl himself considered it to be his masterpiece.

Ralph E. W. Earl (circa 1788–1838)
Oil on canvas, 1836–1837
320 x 236.2 cm. (126 x 93 in.)
National Museum of American Art, Smithsonian Institution; transfer from U.S. District Court for the District of Columbia

CHAPTER 7

Sage of the Hermitage

ON MARCH 4, 1837, ANDREW JACKSON ENDED HIS SECOND TERM AS President. His popularity among the rank and file of Americans was still as strong as ever, as witnessed by the throngs of well-wishers who turned out to bid him farewell. He lived at the Hermitage for the remainder of his life. The worries of executive leadership, particularly the panic of 1837, which had been exacerbated by Jackson's trenchant monetary policies, now rested on the shoulders of his successor, Martin Van Buren. Still, Jackson could not let go. The unsolicited counsel with which he filled his correspondence suggested that part of him still yearned to be in charge.

But in his final years, other concerns closer to home would steal his attention and occupy his energies. The mounting debts of his adopted son, Andrew Jackson, Jr., were seriously jeopardizing the old man's financial security. A brighter note was the fulfillment of an eighteen-year-old promise to his deceased wife, Rachel, that he would become a Christian. On Sunday, July 15, 1838, in a special service at the Hermitage church (which he had built for Rachel in 1823), Jackson joined the Presbyterian faith. A tragic note was the sudden death of his good friend and portraitist, Ralph E. W. Earl, two months later.

Jackson's health began to fail. Although he was able to travel on occasion—such as a visit to New Orleans in January 1840 to celebrate the silver anniversary of his historic victory—it was always taxing. Then in the spring of 1845, he developed massive edema, complaining, "Every time I write I must pause for a breath." Mercifully, the end came soon enough. With his family gathered around his bedside, Jackson died quietly on the evening of June 8, 1845. That summer the nation mourned his passing in eulogies delivered throughout the country.

The Hermitage, Jackson's Tomb, and Andrew J. Donelson's Residence

Samuel B. Jones (active in New York City
1856–1860)
Colored lithograph, 1856
52 x 66.7 cm. (20½ x 26¼ in.)
Prints and Photographs Division, Library of
Congress

THE HERMITAGE JACKSONS TOMB AND ANDREW J. DONELSONS RESIDENCE.
12 MILES FROM NASHVILLE, TENNESSEE.
TAKEN AT THE SPOT MARCH 29TH 1856.

The hero of New Orleans in 1840

Among the artists in New Orleans, R. Brand remains anonymous, except for a signed profile sketch made of Jackson during the latter's visit, on January 8, 1840, to commemorate the Silver Jubilee of the Battle of New Orleans. With crayon and paper, Brand depicted Old Hickory riding in an open carriage, passing a building on a street lined with spectators. The scene is reminiscent of the newspaper reports of the grand welcoming procession of soldiers and citizens that escorted Jackson to the State House, and then to the Place d'Armes (Jackson Square) and St. Louis Cathedral. Along the levee and over Canal and Chartres streets, Jackson rode "*amid a sea* of human heads," in a barouche drawn by four white horses. Balconies were literally white with handkerchiefs waved by ladies; it was "as though at every step of the *cortege,* a thousand snowy and glittering birds were *started, and took wing.*" Jackson bowed in humble acknowledgment. "His head was white," reported the *New-Orleans Commercial Bulletin,* "as if the snow of a hundred winters had fallen upon it; and the palid [*sic*] and wan aspect of his features indicated the near approach of the aged Hero to 'that bourne whence no traveller returns.'"

Somewhere in the throng stood R. Brand, taking note of the great man. The artist was obviously struck with Jackson's weathered appearance: both his stately mien and his feebleness are captured in this amateur sketch, perhaps the only one of its kind that Brand drew.

R. Brand (lifedates unknown)
Ink and crayon on paper, 1840
22.5 x 18.4 cm. (8⅞ x 7¼ in.)
Louisiana State Museum

Andrew Jackson
by Jacques Guillaume
Lucien Amans

In spite of the fact that no portrait of
Jackson was officially commissioned to
commemorate the Silver Jubilee, the
likeness executed by Jacques Guillaume
Lucien Amans has, in retrospect, done
just that. In the 1840s and early 1850s
Amans was the finest portraitist in New
Orleans. Born in Belgium in 1801, he
studied art in Paris, exhibiting in its
salons before sailing to Louisiana in
1836. Virtually unknown outside his
adopted state, Amans won local
recognition for his oil portraits of
Andrew Jackson and Zachary Taylor, the
latter painted from life in 1848.

At the urging of the citizenry, Amans,
on January 10, addressed a letter to the
general requesting a sitting. "If this favor
should be granted by you," wrote the
artist, "my intention is to present the
portrait to the city of New-Orleans." Four
sessions of an hour each would be
sufficient, and Jackson would not need to
interrupt his conversations with friends
and visitors.

The sittings no doubt took place at the
French Exchange Hotel on St. Louis
Street, where a suite of rooms had been
readied for Jackson. The *Courier* reported
that he would receive visitors there
during his visit. There is no way of
knowing just how much time he actually
granted; it was, however, enough for
Amans to paint a careful likeness.
Jackson appears tired, almost exhausted.
The two-week trip from Nashville had
been wearisome for him, not to mention
the plethora of activities scheduled
during his stay. A visit upon his arrival to
the plain of Chalmette, the scene of his
historic battle, had to be postponed
owing to his fatigue.

Jacques Guillaume Lucien Amans
(1801–1888)
Oil on canvas, 1840
153.7 x 125.7 cm. (60½ x 49½ in.)
Historic New Orleans Collection; Museum/
Research Center, Acc. No. 1982.11

Jackson's gold spectacles and case

President Jackson purchased this pair of spectacles from John McAllister & Company of Philadelphia in about 1830. In retirement, and as his eyesight gradually worsened, he began wearing a unique pair of double-lensed glasses whose bifocals folded back along the inside of the frame.

The Hermitage: Home of President Andrew Jackson

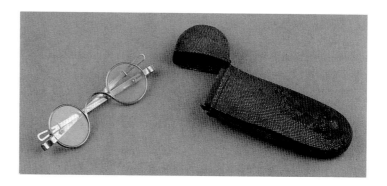

Jackson's white beaver hat

This white beaver hat was "made expressly for His Excellency, Gen'l Andrew Jackson" by Orlando Fish of New York and Washington in about 1829. It became one of Jackson's trademarks and is depicted in many of his portraits. The black "mourning" band was in remembrance of his deceased wife, Rachel.

Tennessee State Museum; Tennessee Historical Society Collection

Andrew Jackson
by Miner Kilbourne Kellogg

This portrait of Jackson was commissioned by a group of Cincinnati Democrats, who selected their townsman Miner Kilbourne Kellogg to call upon the former President at his country residence near Nashville. Sometime in late March of 1840, Kellogg arrived at the Hermitage, where he occupied a room on the second floor and set up his studio in an adjacent chamber. During his prolonged six-week stay, Kellogg painted an insightful likeness. He had the tremendous advantage of being able to observe Jackson in his daily routine over a period of time. The image the old hero projected was one of melancholy. Kellogg perceived it in his conversation, manner, and face. Pensiveness seemed to embody the entire being of this lonely man, who was on the brink of outliving his own era. "These considerations," recalled the artist, "were ever before me and inspired every touch of my pencil."

Kellogg's finished portrait was universally deemed a success. It received high marks from Jackson himself, as well as in the local newspapers. Many of the general's oldest and closest friends— former soldiers and political cronies— considered it the best portrait ever executed of him. Typical was Judge John Catron of Nashville, one of Jackson's last appointees to the bench of the United States Supreme Court. He told Kellogg that he had seen portraits by Jarvis, Earl, and many others, but none could compare to this likeness.

Miner Kilbourne Kellogg (1814–1889)
Oil on canvas, 1840
76.2 x 63.5 cm. (30 x 25 in.)
Cincinnati Art Museum; gift of Charles H. Kellogg, Sr.

Andrew Jackson
by John Wood Dodge

In 1842 miniaturist John Wood Dodge
was in his prime. In Nashville he was
charging about seventy-five dollars for a
small portrait set in a locket or case. By
the end of the year, his receipts totaled
$1,625; he had painted thirty likenesses
of a career total of 545. His portrait of
Jackson was perhaps his most widely
touted work. Dodge had his first sitting
at the Hermitage on March 15, the
general's seventy-fifth birthday, and
completed the likeness on April 8.

The original portrait, a six-inch-square
miniature on ivory (now lost), depicts
Jackson seated, perhaps in his study. The
Nashville Union of April 14, 1842, reported on the painting's spontaneity: *The
first glance at the picture impresses the
spectator with the idea that he had just entered
the apartment of the General who has laid his
book upon the table before him, returned his
spectacles to their case which is held in his left
hand, and is prepared to entertain his friend.*

Dodge painted this smaller head-and-
shoulders version—without any back-
ground or props—for Jackson's close
friend, General Robert Armstrong, who
had assisted him in gaining the initial
sittings.

Dodge's likeness of Jackson appeared
in several engraved versions. It was used
to decorate funeral ribbons, banknotes,
and stamps—the two-cent "Black Jack"
of 1863 proved to be one of the most
popular stamps ever issued by the United
States Post Office.

John Wood Dodge (1807–1893)
Watercolor on ivory, 1842
5.7 x 4.8 cm. (2¼ x 1⅞ in.)
Tennessee State Museum

Photograph of Jackson at the Hermitage shortly before his death

Nothing quite illustrated the link between old and new as tellingly as the modern art of photography. The daguerreotype process, introduced in Paris in the late 1830s and shortly thereafter in the United States, was the invention of Louis Jacques Mandé Daguerre. Images were produced when silver-coated copper plates, sensitized with chemicals, were exposed to sunlight for a regulated period. A mirror image was produced. As a portrait, in the words of one art critic, "the daguerreotype is as near to the living man as we can get. Not even the sensitive paper of the photographic negative intervenes."

In the spring of 1845, Andrew Jackson personally experienced this new phenomenon. He was one of the few veterans of the Revolution to be photographed. He was not, however, the first President to face the camera. Three years before in Boston, John Quincy Adams had sat for his photograph and recalled it being a slow and dull process, which put him to sleep. In spite of his breadth of knowledge, he admitted having no conceivable notion of how the impression emerged upon the plate.

Unfortunately, Jackson made no such observation, leaving the circumstances of this sitting as intriguing as the provenance of this image—it was recently discovered in a box stored in the basement of the Mead Art Museum.

Attributed to Anthony, Edwards & Co.
(active 1842–1847)
Daguerreotype, 1845
13.9 x 10.9 cm. (5½ x 4¼ in.)
Mead Art Museum, Amherst College; gift of William Macbeth, Inc.

The last portrait from life
of Jackson

In the spring of 1845 King Louis-Philippe of France learned that Andrew Jackson was dying. Louis-Philippe desperately wanted a life portrait of Old Hickory to be among those of select American statesmen he was commissioning for his projected historical museum at Versailles. To execute these likenesses, he turned to George Peter Alexander Healy, a promising young American painter who was then working in Paris.

In about mid-May, Healy arrived on the doorstep of the Hermitage. Jackson was still alive. The old man received him pleasantly enough but refused to sit on account of his poor health. "Not for all the kings in Christendom," he exclaimed.

His daughter-in-law, Sarah Yorke, finally persuaded him to change his mind. Thus, what Healy thought had been a futile attempt turned into a visit of several weeks. In that time, he repeatedly gained access to Jackson in his sickroom. Yet now the patient was critical—swollen from his toes to the crown of his head and in bandages to his hips. On one occasion he lamented, "I wish I could do you greater justice as a sitter, Mr. Healy."

Healy somehow managed to finish the portrait at the end of May. Upon its presentation, Jackson examined it for a few minutes before addressing the artist. "I am satisfied, sir, that you stand at the head of your profession. If I may be allowed to judge of my own likeness, I can safely concur in the opinion of my family. This is the best that has been taken."

Before leaving the Hermitage, Healy (still a houseguest when Jackson died) hastily painted a copy portrait for the family. The portrait illustrated here, also painted that year, is believed to have been Healy's personal copy.

George P. A. Healy (1813–1894)
Oil on canvas, 1845
76.5 x 63.8 cm. (30⅛ x 25⅛ in.)
Cummer Gallery of Art; gift of Mr. and Mrs. Algur Meadows

Death of Genl. Andrew Jackson

Like a pebble tossed in a still pond, the news of Jackson's death on June 8, 1845, rippled throughout the nation from small town to large city. Everywhere flags flew at half-mast. Businesses closed. Black suddenly became the national color, as banners of mourning decorated everything from newspaper columns to government edifices. In conversations, almost no one referred to the deceased by his proper name. Somehow such epithets as "Old Hickory" and "Hero of New Orleans" seemed more endearing. In the weeks following, dozens of eulogists in speech after speech recalled his illustrious career as warrior and statesman. They rationalized his shortcomings and glorified his victories. He was compared with history's most celebrated commanders, from Hannibal to Napoleon, and was deemed to be superior to them all, save for the immortal Washington.

This nationwide observance of mourning took many forms, including souvenir lithographs depicting Jackson's death. Nathaniel Currier alone published at least four similar scenes. A typical portrayal was of Jackson lying in bed with his hand resting on an open Bible. Watching over him are four figures whose identities can only be surmised. Based on the reminiscences of the granddaughter, Rachel Jackson Lawrence, her father and mother and Dr. John H. Esselman were among those present. Rachel, then a girl of twelve, stood at the foot of the bed, her hands near her grandfather's feet and her eyes fixed on his still face.

Nathaniel Currier (1813–1888)
Hand-colored lithograph, 1845
30 x 21.7 cm. (11¹³⁄₁₆ x 8⁹⁄₁₆ in.)
National Portrait Gallery, Smithsonian Institution

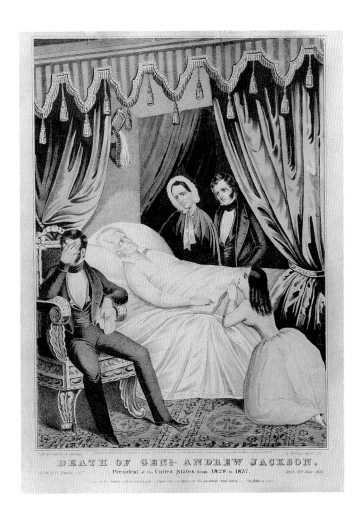

Invitation to Jackson's funeral

On Tuesday, June 10, 1845, Jackson was buried beside his wife, Rachel, in the columned mausoleum he had erected in the garden adjacent to the house. An estimated gathering of three thousand mourners, arriving in more than two hundred carriages and on countless horses, attended that morning's services.

Private collection

Andrew Jackson memorial ribbons

These silk memorial ribbons, recalling Jackson's glory as patriot, statesman, and hero, include images after his portraits by James Barton Longacre, John Wood Dodge, Ralph E. W. Earl, and William James Hubard.

Silk, 1845
Private collection

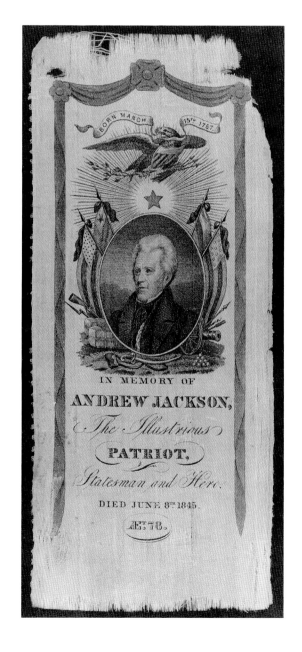

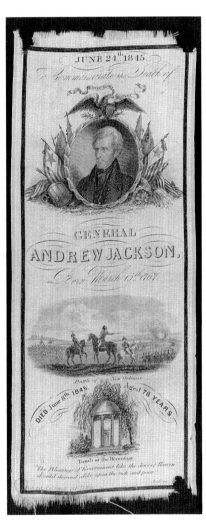

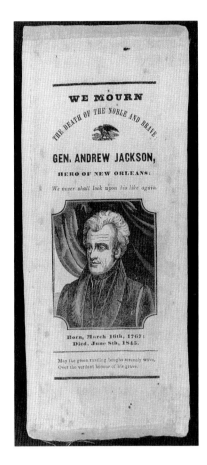

Andrew Jackson, Jr.

Andrew and Rachel Jackson never had children of their own. In 1808 they adopted a twin boy born to Rachel's sister-in-law, Elizabeth Donelson, whose delicate health prevented her from nursing two babies. They named him Andrew Jackson, Jr. (1808–1865). From the start, fatherhood mellowed Jackson's streak of bellicosity. But as the lad reached maturity, he began to test his father's patience as no other person had ever done. In spite of repeated parental exhortations, young Andrew indulged in a lifelong practice of spending freely and incurring large debts. In later years, the President was obliged to accept generous loans from friends to cover his son's ill-advised business dealings and land speculations. But the trend still contin-ued, until Andrew, Jr., had squandered his father's entire sizeable estate. In 1856, with debts of nearly $100,000, he had little recourse but to sell the Hermitage to the state of Tennessee.

Neither ambitious nor remotely intellectually curious, Andrew, Jr., seemed to be happiest in the field hunting, with gun in hand, as depicted in this portrait by Ralph E. W. Earl. Tragically, this pursuit proved to be his end. In April 1865, just a few days after Lee surrendered to Grant at Appomattox Courthouse, Virginia, Andrew acciden-tally shot himself in the hand while climbing over a fence. He died of lockjaw at the age of fifty-seven.

Ralph E. W. Earl (circa 1788–1838)
Oil on canvas, circa 1833
74.9 x 59.7 cm. (29½ x 23½ in.)
The Hermitage: Home of President Andrew Jackson

Sarah Yorke Jackson

By the autumn of 1831, President Jackson had learned to question many of the decisions of his incorrigible and impulsive son, Andrew Jackson, Jr. For one thing, the twenty-two-year-old suitor seemed to be perpetually falling in love. When he planned on marrying Sarah Yorke (1805–1887) that November, the President had strong reservations, which he mostly kept to himself. Although he understood that Sarah was three years older than Andrew and was the orphaned daughter of a successful Philadelphia merchant, he had no personal knowledge of her family and could only trust his son's judgment.

Yet Jackson quickly came to favor this union, after meeting his amiable daughter-in-law. The newlyweds lived in the White House for a brief time, but when Sarah first became pregnant in 1832, the couple moved to the Hermitage, where they spent the remainder of their married lives. More than just a welcome addition to the family, Sarah proved to be a joy and comfort to Jackson in his old age. She nursed him in ill health and became the mainstay of the household.

Ralph E. W. Earl (circa 1788–1838)
Oil on canvas, circa 1833
74.9 x 62.2 cm. (29½ x 24½ in.)
The Hermitage: Home of President Andrew Jackson

Prototype likeness for the twenty-dollar bill

With the exception of Ralph E. W. Earl, Thomas Sully executed more images of Old Hickory than any other artist. His register of paintings listed eleven, three of which he painted in the spring and summer of 1845. These three were all based upon this portrait, believed to have been executed in 1824. Allegedly Sully presented this earlier work to Jackson, who in turn gave it to Francis P. Blair, an influential member of the Kitchen Cabinet. Blair always claimed, mistakenly, that this was Sully's original life portrait, painted when Jackson visited Philadelphia in 1819, soon after the close of the Seminole War. In 1852 Blair loaned the painting to George W. Childs of Philadelphia, who published an engraving made from it by Thomas B. Welch. Today the image is most easily recognized as the prototype for the twenty-dollar bill.

Thomas Sully (1783–1872)
Oil on canvas, circa 1824
51.8 x 43.8 cm. (20⅜ x 17¼ in.)
National Gallery of Art; Andrew W. Mellon Collection

Five-dollar United States Treasury note, 1869 "rainbow series"

Unknown to Thomas Sully, his circa 1824 likeness of Old Hickory was to become ubiquitous. On December 22, 1866, Spencer M. Clark, the first head of the United States Bureau of Engraving and Printing, ordered an engraved series of heads of the former Presidents. To execute these oval portraits, designed for paper currency, he consulted Alfred Sealey, a reputable engraver with the National Bank Note Company of New York. Clark wanted to begin the series with Jackson's image. Allowing for some modifications, he suggested that Sealey copy a popular engraving by Moseley Isaac Danforth after Dodge's miniature of 1842.

Inexplicably, the Dodge-Danforth likeness was rejected. On January 11, 1867, Clark sent Sealey four photographs, reduced to a desired size, of Sully's circa 1824 head image of Jackson. Confident that Sealey would readily determine any necessary modifications to make in his engraving, Clark specified only that he should continue the form and drapery of Jackson's torso down to the bottom of the oval border. Sealey accomplished this in part by depicting Jackson clutching his cloak in his hand.

Sealey's engraving first appeared in 1869 on the five-dollar United States note. Because of the bill's distinctive multicolored design, it was designated the "rainbow series." Although copied by subsequent engravers, the Sealey-Sully likeness of Jackson has decorated a variety of federal notes, including the ten-thousand-dollar bill of 1878, the ten-dollar bill of the early 1900s, and the twenty-dollar bill of today.

Norman Brand

Andrew Jackson by Thomas Sully

On July 8, 1845, a month to the day after Jackson died, Sully began this full-length, life-size portrait of the hero of New Orleans. The likeness was after Sully's "head" portraits painted in April and June. When he completed it on July 31, Sully had created Jackson's most dashing likeness. That year he exhibited it at the joint exhibition of the Artists' Fund Society of Philadelphia and the Pennsylvania Academy of the Fine Arts.

Sully received eight hundred dollars for this painting, whose provenance traces back to Samuel Phillips Lee, an in-law of the Blair family. Lee was the son of the noted Revolutionary War general, "Lighthorse Harry" Lee. In 1843, he married Francis P. Blair's only daughter, Elizabeth. Subsequently the portrait passed through several owners, finally ending up in the collection of William Wilson Corcoran.

Thomas Sully (1783–1872)
Oil on canvas, 1845
247 x 156.2 cm. (97¼ x 61½ in.)
The Corcoran Gallery; gift of William Wilson Corcoran, 1869

Andrew Jackson
by Clark Mills

Jackson's death rekindled America's
interest in erecting a grand equestrian
statue to one of her foremost patriots.
The country could not yet boast an
equestrian monument, not even to the
beloved Washington. After the Jackson
Monument Committee was formed in
Washington in September 1845, it
launched a national subscription drive
and invited artists' proposals. In 1848
Clark Mills, a talented young sculptor
living in Charleston, South Carolina,
submitted the winning entry. His small
plaster model portrayed Jackson on a
rearing horse in the act of reviewing his
troops just prior to the Battle of New
Orleans. Then, after four years of
painstaking modeling and casting, Mills
completed his larger-than-life bronze
statue and placed it upon a marble
pedestal in Lafayette Square, opposite
the White House, in time for the grand
unveiling on January 8, 1853, the thirty-
eighth anniversary of Jackson's historic
victory.

This statuette of Mills's colossal
monument was one of a limited number
patented in 1855 by Cornelius and Baker
of Philadelphia.

Clark Mills (1815–1883)
Pot metal, circa 1855
66 cm. (26 in.)
National Portrait Gallery, Smithsonian
Institution; gift of Mr. and Mrs. John L.
Sanders in memory of William Monroe Geer

NOTES ON SOURCES

Introduction
"[Jackson] is certainly the most popular man," Philip Hone, *The Diary of Philip Hone, 1828–1851*, ed. Allan Nevins (New York, 1927), vol. 1, pp. 96–97.

Chapter 1: Before Glory
"Every step he took," Thomas Hart Benton, *Thirty Years View; or, A History of the Working of the American Government for Thirty Years, from 1820 to 1850* (New York, 1856), vol. 1, p. 738. For the Russell Bean anecdote see James Parton, *Life of Andrew Jackson* (New York, 1861), vol. 1, pp. 228–29.

Chapter 2: The Iron General
The popular story of Jackson sharing his acorns with the soldier is from Parton, *Jackson*, vol. 1, pp. 446–47. "I am in your power," quoted in Robert V. Remini, *Andrew Jackson* (New York, 1977–1984), vol. 1, pp. 218–19. "Without the personal firmness," quoted in Parton, *Jackson*, vol. 1, p. 498.

Chapter 3: Hero of New Orleans
"As a testimony of the high sense," quoted in Remini, *Andrew Jackson*, vol. 1, p. 295. "It is so unlike the portraits," Parton, *Jackson*, vol. 2, pp. 327–28. "Persons desirous of obtaining," *Louisiana Gazette* (New Orleans), May 6, 1815.

Chapter 4: "See the Conquering Hero Comes"
For Jackson's portrait sittings to Peale, see Charles Willson Peale Diary, January 29–30, 1819, Peale-Sellers Papers, American Philosophical Society, Philadelphia. "The board is met," *New York Evening Post*, March 11, 1819. "I have just been to see," Andrew Jackson, *Correspondence of Andrew Jackson*, ed. John Spencer Bassett (Washington, D.C., 1926–1935), vol. 6, p. 471.

Chapter 5: The Presidential Chair
"Poor Adams used to visit," Hone, *Diary*, vol. 1, p. 97. For Binns's own account of the coffin handbill, see John Binns, *Recollections of the Life of John Binns: Twenty-nine Years in Europe and Fifty-three in the United States* (Philadelphia, 1854), pp. 243, 245–46, 255–56. "I had rather be a doorkeeper," quoted in Remini, *Andrew Jackson*, vol. 2, p. 149.

Chapter 6: President Jackson
"[Jackson] has very little the appearance," James Stuart, *Three Years in North America* (Edinburgh, 1833), vol. 2, p. 43. "No one could tell," Seba Smith, *Letters Written During the President's Tour, 'Down East,' by Myself, Major Jack Downing, of Downingville* (Cincinnati, Ohio, 1833), p. 46. "Though we live under," quoted in Arthur M. Schlesinger, Jr., *The Age of Jackson* (Boston, 1945), p. 110. "The President's *thinking* machine," quoted in *ibid.*, p. 73. "Rotation in office," quoted in Remini, *Andrew Jackson*, vol. 2, p. 183. "A bag of meal," quoted in *ibid.*, vol. 3, p. 3. *"But I will kill it!"* quoted in John C. Fitzpatrick, ed., *Annual Report of the American Historical Association for the Year 1918. . . . The Autobiography of Martin Van Buren* (Washington, D.C., 1920), vol. 2, p. 625 (hereafter cited as Van Buren, *Autobiography*). "Had the ship been at," quoted in *Niles' Weekly Register*, March 21, 1835. "Make me as I am," quoted in C. Edwards Lester, *The Artist, the Merchant, and the Statesman, of the Age of the Medici, and of Our Own Times* (New York, 1845), vol. 1, pp. 65–66. "Mr. Powers has succeeded," *Cincinnati Daily Gazette*, February 5, 1835. "Sitting with one of Major Donelson's," Van Buren, *Autobiography*, vol. 2, p. 353. "His face is unlike any other," quoted in Parton, *Jackson*, vol. 3, p. 598.

Chapter 7: Sage of the Hermitage
"Every time I write," Andrew Jackson to Francis P. Blair, May 3, 1845, Andrew Jackson Papers, Library of Congress, Washington, D.C. *"Amid a sea* of human heads," *New-Orleans Commercial Bulletin*, January 10, 1840. "His head was white," *ibid.* "If this favor should be granted," Amans to Jackson, January 10, 1840, Jackson Papers, Library of Congress. "These considerations," in "Miner K. Kellogg Reminiscences," New Harmony Collection, Indiana Historical Society Library, Indianapolis. "The daguerreotype is as near," Charles Henry Hart, "Life Portraits of Andrew Jackson," *McClure's Magazine* 9 (July 1897): 803. "Not for all the kings," George P. A. Healy, *Reminiscences of a Portrait Painter* (Chicago, 1894), p. 139. "I wish I could do you greater justice," *ibid.*, p. 142. "I am satisfied, sir," quoted in Parton, *Jackson*, vol. 3, p. 673.

SUGGESTED READINGS

Davison, Nancy Reynolds. "E. W. Clay: American Political Caricaturist of the Jacksonian Era." Ph.D. diss., University of Michigan, 1980.

Hart, Charles Henry. "Life Portraits of Andrew Jackson." *McClure's Magazine* 9 (July 1897): 795–804.

Jackson, Andrew. *Correspondence of Andrew Jackson.* Edited by John Spencer Bassett. 7 vols. Washington, D.C., 1926–1935.

————. *The Papers of Andrew Jackson.* Edited by Harold D. Moser *et al.* 2 vols. to date. Knoxville, Tenn., 1980–.

James, Marquis. *The Life of Andrew Jackson, Complete in One Volume.* Indianapolis, Ind., 1938.

Parton, James. *Life of Andrew Jackson.* 3 vols. New York, 1861.

Reid, John, and John Henry Eaton. *The Life of Andrew Jackson.* Philadelphia, 1817.

Remini, Robert V. *Andrew Jackson and the Course of American Empire, 1767–1821; American Freedom, 1822–1832; American Democracy, 1833–1845.* 3 vols. New York, 1977–1984.

Schlesinger, Arthur M., Jr. *The Age of Jackson.* Boston, 1945.

Ward, John William. *Andrew Jackson, Symbol for an Age.* New York, 1962.

ADDITIONAL OBJECTS IN THE EXHIBITION

Before Glory

Andrew Jackson
Unidentified artist
Ivory cameo brooch, not dated
3.5 x 2.2 cm. (1⅜ x ⅞ in.)
National Museum of American History,
Smithsonian Institution

Marriage bond of Andrew Jackson and
Rachel Donelson Robards, January 7,
1794
Tennessee State Library and Archives

Proclamation commissioning Jackson a
judge of the Tennessee Superior Court,
Knoxville, December 22, 1798
Tennessee State Library and Archives

Letter from John Sevier to Andrew
Jackson requesting Jackson to select a
dueling ground, October 1803
Tennessee State Library and Archives

The Iron General

Jackson's writing kit and inkwell used
during the Creek War
Tennessee State Museum; Tennessee
Historical Society Collection

Jackson's leather wallet
The Hermitage: Home of President
Andrew Jackson; on permanent loan to
the Tennessee State Museum

Hero of New Orleans

Andrew Jackson
Ralph E. W. Earl (circa 1788–1838)
Oil on canvas, 1818
240 x 146.7 cm. (94½ x 57¾ in.)
Tennessee State Museum

*The Taking of the City of Washington in
America*
Unidentified artist
Engraving, 1814
42.9 x 52.7 cm. (16⅞ x 20¾ in.)
Prints and Photographs Division, Library
of Congress

John Bull Before New Orleans
William Charles (1776–1820)
Etching and aquatint, 1815
23.2 x 33.9 cm. (9⅛ x 13⅜ in.)
American Antiquarian Society

Defeat of the British Army, 12,000 strong . . .
Philibert-Louis Debucourt (1755–1832),
after Hyacinthe Laclotte
Engraving, 1817
53.9 x 68.6 cm. (21¼ x 27 in.)
Tennessee State Museum

Treaty of Peace
Broadsheet, 1815
Historic New Orleans Collection

*Answer Tendered To the District Court of the
United States By Major General Jackson . . . ,*
New Orleans, 1815
Rare Book and Special Collections
Division, Library of Congress

The Life of Andrew Jackson by John Reid
and John Henry Eaton, Philadelphia,
1817
Private collection

*Historical Memoir of the War in West Florida
and Louisiana in 1814–15. With an Atlas,*
by Major A. Lacarriere Latour,
Philadelphia, 1816
Historic New Orleans Collection

Jackson's knife, fork, and spoon set used
during the New Orleans campaign
Tennessee State Museum; Tennessee
Historical Society Collection

"See the Conquering Hero Comes"

James Monroe, 1758–1831
John Vanderlyn (1755–1852)
Oil on canvas, 1816
67.3 x 56.8 cm. (26½ x 22⅜ in.)
National Portrait Gallery, Smithsonian
Institution

Andrew Jackson
James B. Longacre (1794–1869), after
Thomas Sully
Stipple engraving, proof, 1819–1820
37.5 x 30 cm. (14¾ x 11¹³⁄₁₆ in.)
National Portrait Gallery, Smithsonian
Institution

*American Justice!! or The Ferocious Yankee
Genl. Jack's Reward for Butchering Two
British Subjects!!!*
Unidentified artist
Hand-colored engraving, 1819
24.8 x 34.9 cm. (9¾ x 13¾ in.)
Tennessee State Museum

The Presidential Chair

Uncle Alfred Jackson, circa 1813–1901
W. G. and A. J. Thuss Photographic
Gallery (active circa 1889–1931)
Gelatin silver print, circa 1890
13.9 x 9.8 cm. (5½ x 3⅞ in.)
The Hermitage: Home of President
Andrew Jackson

"House Hannah" Jackson,
circa 1801–circa 1895
W. G. and A. J. Thuss Photographic
Gallery (active circa 1889–1931)
Albumen print, circa 1889
14.6 x 9.8 cm. (5¾ x 3⅞ in.)
The Hermitage: Home of President
Andrew Jackson

Copper lusterware pitcher with image of
"General Jackson, The Hero of New
Orleans," circa 1828, after Joseph Wood
20.9 cm. (8¼ in.)
National Museum of American History,
Smithsonian Institution

Plate with image of "General Jackson,
The Hero of New Orleans," circa 1828,
after Joseph Wood
22.2 cm. (8¾ in.) diameter
National Museum of American History,
Smithsonian Institution

The Man! The Jack Ass
James Akin (circa 1773–1846)
Lithograph, not dated
27.3 x 12.1 cm. (10¾ x 4¾ in.)
American Antiquarian Society

Published letter of John Overton, April 3,
1824, concerning the circumstances of
Jackson's marriage
Broadside, 1827
Rare Book and Special Collections
Division, Library of Congress

A *Brief Account of some of the Bloody Deeds of
General Jackson*
Handbill, 1828
Private collection

An Address of Henry Clay, to the Public . . . ,
Washington, D.C., 1827
Rare Book and Special Collections
Division, Library of Congress

*Reminiscences; or An Extract from the
Catalogue of General Jackson's 'Juvenile
Indiscretions,' Between the Ages of 23 and 60*
by James L. Armstrong, New York,
circa 1828
Rare Book and Special Collections
Division, Library of Congress

The Jackson Wreath, or National Souvenir by
James M'Henry, Philadelphia, 1829
Merl M. Moore, Jr.

"Stop the Runaway"
Reproduction of an original newspaper
advertisement in the *Tennessee Gazette*
(Nashville), October 3, 1804

President Jackson

Andrew Jackson
James Barton Longacre (1794–1869)
Sepia watercolor on artist board, 1829
25.6 x 20.2 cm. (10 1/16 x 7 15/16 in.)
National Portrait Gallery, Smithsonian
Institution

Vase with portrait of Jackson, after James
B. Longacre
Tucker and Hemphill, Philadelphia
Porcelain, circa 1832
29.5 cm. (11 5/8 in.)
The White House Collection

Andrew Jackson, President of the United States
Albert Newsam (1809–1864), after
William James Hubard
Lithograph, 1830
49.8 x 35.6 cm. (19 5/8 x 14 in.)
National Portrait Gallery, Smithsonian
Institution

Thomas Hart Benton, 1782–1858
Ferdinand Thomas Lee Boyle
(1820–1906)
Oil on canvas, circa 1861
91.4 x 73.7 cm. (36 x 29 in.)
National Portrait Gallery, Smithsonian
Institution

William Learned Marcy, 1786–1857
Unidentified artist
Oil on canvas, not dated
87.3 x 73.7 cm. (34 3/8 x 29 in.)
National Portrait Gallery, Smithsonian
Institution; gift of Joseph Collector

The Globe
Broadside, subscription list, 1830
Rare Book and Special Collections
Division, Library of Congress

*Letter from Mrs. [Mary] Barney to Gen.
Jackson*
Silk broadside, 1829
Rare Book and Special Collections
Division, Library of Congress

Jackson's Veto, on the United States Bank
Silk broadside, 1832
Rare Book and Special Collections
Division, Library of Congress

*,00001—The value of a unit with four
cyphers going before it*
Edward Williams Clay (1799–1857)
Lithograph, 1831
39.4 x 29.2 cm. (15 1/2 x 11 1/2 in.)
The Library Company of Philadelphia

The Grand National Caravan Moving East
George Endicott and Moses Swett
Lithography Company (active
1830–1834)
Lithograph, 1833
22.9 x 36.5 cm. (9 x 14 3/8 in.)
Prints and Photographs Division, Library
of Congress

*"The Government." "[I] Take the
Responsibility"*
George Endicott and Moses Swett
Lithography Company (active 1830–
1834)
Hand-colored lithograph, 1834
21.6 x 33.7 cm. (8 1/2 x 13 1/4 in.)
Prints and Photographs Division, Library
of Congress

Symptoms of a Locked Jaw
David Claypoole Johnston (1799–1865)
Lithograph, 1834
31.1 x 22.9 cm. (12 1/4 x 9 in.)
Tennessee State Library and Archives

*The Decapitation of a great Blockhead by the
Mysterious agency of the Claret coloured Coat*
Unidentified artist
Lithograph, 1834
30.9 x 45.1 cm. (12 13/16 x 17 3/4 in.)
Prints and Photographs Division, Library
of Congress

Cash Payment—Arrival of the French Cavalry
Henry R. Robinson Lithography
Company (active 1831–1851)
Hand-colored lithograph, 1836
28.9 x 46 cm. (11 3/8 x 18 1/8 in.)
The Library Company of Philadelphia

Fifty Cents Shin Plaster
Henry R. Robinson Lithography
Company (active 1831–1851)
Lithograph, 1837
26.7 x 44.3 cm. (10½ x 17⁷⁄₁₆ in.)
Prints and Photographs Division, Library
of Congress

Treasury Note 75 Cents
Napoleon Sarony (1821–1896)
Hand-colored lithograph, 1837
24.8 x 44.1 cm. (9¾ x 17⅜ in.)
American Antiquarian Society

The Times
Edward Williams Clay (1799–1857)
Lithograph, 1837
32.7 x 48.3 cm. (12⅞ x 19 in.)
National Museum of American History,
Smithsonian Institution; Peters
Collection

Sage of the Hermitage

Andrew Jackson
Trevor Thomas Fowler (active
1829–1869)
Oil on canvas, 1840
76.8 x 63.5 cm. (30¼ x 25 in.)
National Portrait Gallery, Smithsonian
Institution

Andrew Jackson
James Tooley, Jr. (1816–1844), after
Edward D. Marchant
Watercolor on ivory, 1840
10.8 x 8.6 cm. (4¼ x 3⅜ in.)
National Portrait Gallery, Smithsonian
Institution; gift of Mr. William H. Lively,
Mrs. Mary Lively Hoffman, and Dr.
Charles J. Lively

Andrew Jackson
Adolphe Lafosse (circa 1810–1879), after
daguerreotype attributed to Mathew
Brady
Lithograph with tintstone, 1856
54.5 x 43.5 cm. (21⁷⁄₁₆ x 17⅛ in.)
National Portrait Gallery, Smithsonian
Institution

*The Last Likeness Taken of Andrew
Jackson . . .*
Moseley Isaac Danforth (1800–1862),
after John Wood Dodge
Engraving, 1843
26.4 x 20.6 cm. (10⅜ x 8⅛ in.)
National Portrait Gallery, Smithsonian
Institution

*Mill's Colossal Equestrian Statue of General
Andrew Jackson*
Thomas S. Sinclair (active 1830–1870)
Colored lithograph, 1853
44.5 x 55.6 cm. (17½ x 21⅞ in.)
Private collection

25th Anniversary of the Battle of New-Orleans
Silk ribbon, 1840
Historic New Orleans Collection;
Museum/Research Center, Acc. No.
1974.67

Horse-handle presentation sword and
scabbard, 1834–1835
The Hermitage: Home of President
Andrew Jackson

Jackson's cane
The Hermitage: Home of President
Andrew Jackson

Jackson's Bible
The Hermitage: Home of President
Andrew Jackson

The Weekly Herald, New York, June 28,
1845
Private collection

INDEX

Photography credits
Jan White Brantley: 6, 22, 39, 53, 65
(Monumental Inscriptions!), 104, 105
June Dorman: 4, 26, 27, 65 *(The Pedlar and His Pack),* 68, 80, 106 (hat), 108
Jerry Ferrin: cover
Tom Liddell: 25, 32, 71, 77, 97, 106 (spectacles), 114, 115
McLaughlin Studios & Associates: 99
Rolland White: 34, 40, 56 (Vanderlyn portrait), 62, 64, 75, 78, 81, 82, 87, 88, 111, 112, 113, 117, 120

Edited by Frances K. Stevenson
and Dru Dowdy

Designed and composed by Polly Sexton, Washington, D.C., and electronically typeset in Adobe New Baskerville and Caslon Old Style by Unicorn Graphics, Washington, D.C.

Printed on eighty-pound Warren's Lustro Offset Enamel cream with Strathmore Americana endsheets by Garamond/Pridemark Press, Inc., Baltimore, Maryland